Seasoned
with Grace

Eldress Bertha Lindsay, in the Trustees' Office kitchen, 1986. *Bruce Alexander, photographer.*

Seasoned with Grace

My Generation of Shaker Cooking

By Eldress Bertha Lindsay

Edited by Mary Rose Boswell

The Countryman Press
Woodstock, Vermont

FIRST PRINTING

Cover and text design by James Brisson,
Williamsville, Vermont
Frontispiece and cover photographs by
Bruce Alexander, Chester, New Hampshire
Typesetting by the F. W. Roberts Company,
Belfast, Maine
Printed in the United States of America

Library of Congress Cataloging-in-Publication Data

Lindsay, Bertha, b. 1894.
Seasoned with grace.

Bibliography: p.
Includes index.
1. Cookery, Shaker. I. Boswell, Mary Rose.
II. Title.
TX715.L75856   1987   641.5′088287   87-19933
ISBN 0-88150-099-2 (pbk.)

0 9 8 7 6 5 4 3 2 1

CONTENTS

PREFACE

One may wonder about the appearance of yet another Shaker cookbook when a variety have already been published. Many of these, however, deal with the nineteenth century, and most of their recipes come from manuscripts gathered from different communities. Many of the cookbooks give an idealized picture based on secondary sources.[1] Three Canterbury cookbooks have been available to the public, and they reflect how one Society dined, but do not indicate how or when the dishes were used.[2] Bertha Lindsay's cookbook, which focuses on the eighty years she has lived at the village, provides more information about Shaker cooking than has been previously published.

This work is the result of Eldress Bertha's wish to record the culinary traditions of the Canterbury Shaker Society, a community that has not been studied to the extent that some of the others have. The comparative lack of attention given to this village is surprising, since it is one of two remaining active communities,[3] and it has played, and continues to play, a significant role in the history of the Shakers. Eldress Bertha is the ideal person to tell the story because she grew up at the village and never left it. Her entire life has revolved around serving and representing her community as a cook, and although her eyesight was drastically impaired in 1982, she still maintains her traditional role. The text of this book is based on taped interviews and monologues, so the main story is told from her point of view. She selected each recipe, and no material was included without her permission. Some of the recipes were chosen because they are examples of traditional ways of cooking. Many were passed down to her orally and were probably so routine that no one had ever bothered to record them before in writing. Others were included because they proved to be popular over the years. Still others were chosen because they were "different" or were a challenge to try. This collection gives us, then, a portrait of Bertha as a twentieth-century Shaker cook and an intimate view of the evolving culinary traditions at the Canterbury community.

My part in this project was to solicit volunteers to transcribe the tapes and test the recipes. I also organized the material. In preparing her book, Bertha initially recorded three monologues; these included an introduction and several essays. Because more text was needed, I listened to additional tapes that she had recorded for other projects and interviewed her again.[4] Except for a few grammatical changes, her wording was kept intact. To check accuracy, I read diaries and journals written by other Canterbury Shakers. In almost all cases, Bertha's recall for dates, events, and names was perfect. To give a historical context to her story, I added the chronology, map, biographies, and the chapter on dietary traditions.

Testing the recipes was the biggest hurdle in compiling the cookbook. Many of the recipes came from notebooks, scraps of paper, and Bertha's memory. Some of the recipes were written to feed a great number of people. Some omitted quantities altogether. Because Bertha was so familiar with these recipes, she assumed that proportions were easy to "fill in." To avoid error, a group of volunteers, including myself, made the dishes, following her instructions. We frequently called on her for advice and always took the final product to her for approval. When a dish passed inspection—for she knew exactly how it should taste—we recorded the proportions used. Occasionally we noted our own recommendations when we thought a modern cook might want to make additional changes.

Although I have added some reference material to give background to her text, this book is Bertha's work.

—*M.R.B.*

ACKNOWLEDGMENTS

Many people generously contributed to this book and aided in its completion: Galen Beale, Rita Braskie, John Cunha, Carolyn Davidson, Janet Deranian, Virginia Dudley, Renée E. Fox, Marge Gibbs, Lora Smith Goss, Leah Gowen, Marcia Byrom Hartwell, Sister Ethel Hudson, Jean McMahon Humez, Adaline Kathmann, Richard Kathmann, Sarah Kinter, Sue Kowalski, Betty Ladd, Helen Love, Richard A. Morse, Esq., Adelaide Peale, Sharon Rask, Leona Merrill Rowell, Mary Ann Sanborn, Gerri Shakra, Norma Smith, Eldress Gertrude Soule, June Sprigg, David R. Starbuck, Nola Stokes, Charles "Bud" Thompson, Margaretta Thompson, Judith Wildman, Langdon G. Wright, Helen A. Zietz.

The following have kindly granted permission to quote from published works:

Family Circle Inc., for permission to quote from *Family Circle Magazine* (December 1965).

MacMillan Company for permission to quote from Amy Bess Miller and Persis Wellington Fuller, *The Best of Shaker Cooking,* 1970.

Pleasant Hill Press for permission to quote from Elizabeth C. Kremer, *We Make You Kindly Welcome: Recipes from Trustees' House Daily Fare,* 1970.

Herald Press for permission to quote from Mary Emma Showalter, *Mennonite Community Cookbook: Favorite Family Recipes,* 1950.

IDENTIFYING THE
SHAKERS

*T*he Shaker sect entered the American scene in 1774, when a group of eight converts sailed from England to New York to start a new ministry. While the rest of the country's colonists were contemplating war, the Shakers, led by Ann Lee, began preaching their religious beliefs throughout New England. The members practiced celibacy and regarded their leader, whom they called "Mother Ann," as a prophet and the second coming of the Christ spirit.[1] The sect was formally known as the "United Society of Believers in Christ's Second Appearing," but the term "Shaker," which referred to the early members' charismatic practices, became the common name. By 1898 twenty-four communities had been founded in New England, New York, Georgia, Florida, Indiana, Ohio, and Kentucky. Most communities had closed by the turn of the century, however, and only two remain active today: Canterbury, NH, and Sabbathday Lake, ME.[2]

The community at New Lebanon, New York, founded in 1787, became the seat of the Lead Ministry, which advised the entire sect. Groups of two or three communities in one geographic area formed bishoprics, led by Elders and

Eldresses. Communities were composed of Families, each usually consisting of fewer than one hundred members and having its own dwelling house, mills, buildings, and industries. The Church, or Center, Family, also had a meetinghouse where all members of that community attended service. At least one Family was set aside for Novitiates, or potential converts. Each Family was governed by Elders and Eldresses who took charge of the spiritual concerns; Deacons and Deaconesses who supervised the daily activities; and Trustees and Office Sisters who took care of the business transactions with the "World." The Church Family Elders and Eldresses were responsible for the entire community.[3]

The Canterbury Shakers began gathering in New Hampshire in 1782. Sent by Mother Ann, Israel Chauncy and Ebenezer Cooley preached at a meetinghouse a few miles from the town of Canterbury to "open the testimony of the second appearing of Christ." The two missionaries spoke on the confession of sins, self-denial, and separation from the "World."[4] Ten years later, the Canterbury Society was formally established, the fifth of the Shaker communities. The following year, the Enfield Society was founded about forty miles northwest. These two villages formed the New

Plate 1. Canterbury Shaker Village, looking northeast at the Meeting House and the Dwelling House, 1982. *Todd Smith, photographer.*

Hampshire bishopric and answered to the Lead Ministry in New Lebanon. The Canterbury Shakers created four Families: the Church; the Second, located due north; he North, located farther north and home of the Novitiate order; and the West, a short-lived Family that also housed potential converts and was under the care of the North Family.

Although the Canterbury Society remained comparatively small—its membership never reached more than three hundred at a time—the village became important for several reasons. The Canterbury community was blessed with good, efficient leaders, and it became known for the high quality of its agricultural products and animals. Several of its industries were successful, including the manufacture and sale of cloaks, sweaters, herbal medicines, and washing machines. For a time the Canterbury Shakers were responsible for printing the sect's periodicals and books. As other communities closed, some of the remaining members and property moved to Canterbury. In 1957 the village became the seat of the Lead Ministry, and it remains active today with three female members.

Plate 2.   Trustees' Office, east entrance, looking south, 1982. *Todd Smith, photographer.*

CANTERBURY SHAKER VILLAGE CHRONOLOGY

1774 Ann Lee (1736–1784), founder of Shakerism, and 7 followers leave England to escape religious persecution. They sail to New York to begin a new ministry.

1782 "Mother Ann," as she is known, sends Ebenezer Cooley and Israel Chauncy to New Hampshire to conduct missionary efforts there. Members gather at the Whitcher farm.

1792 The Canterbury Society is formally established with 43 members. Eventually 4 Families are organized.

1795 Canterbury Shakers begin planting orchards and erect a mill for grinding corn and grain.

1800 There are 41 Brothers and 42 Sisters living at the Church Family.

1801 The dairy and cider businesses start at this time.

1821 The Lead Ministry in New Lebanon, New York, issues the first written regulations regarding the consumption of food and drink.

1824 The Canterbury Shakers begin selling herbs for medicinal purposes.

1829 The Canterbury Shakers begin selling garden seeds.

1835 The Canterbury Shakers publish their first "Catalogue of Medicinal Plants and Vegetable Medicines." It lists 146 herbs and 16 extracts, oils, and ointments for sale.

1841 The distillery is moved and enlarged to encompass the production of sarsaparilla syrup. The Lead Ministry advises the Shaker societies to restrain their consumption of pork, cider, tea, and coffee.

1844 By this time, Canterbury has become one of the main printing centers among the Shaker communities.

1847 The Canterbury Shakers issue their second herbal catalogue. They list, for the first time, "sweet herbs" packaged in cannisters: sweet marjoram, summer savory, sage, and thyme. These herbs are sold for culinary purposes.

1849 The Canterbury Shakers begin selling rose water. It is manufactured at the village until about 1865.

1850 There are 58 Brothers and 85 Sisters living at the Church Family.

1854 The Canterbury Shakers publish their fourth and last herbal catalogue. It lists 146 herbs, 5 syrups, 16 extracts, and 4 sweet herbs.

1861 Tea drinking is reintroduced at the village.

1862 The Canterbury Shakers begin raising swine again.

1875 Membership in the Church Family includes 34 Brothers and 79 Sisters.

1876 The Shaker Washing Machine and Corbett's Compound Concentrated Syrup of Sarsaparilla, both sold by the Canterbury Shakers, receive gold medals at the Centennial Exhibition in Philadelphia.

1882 *Mary Whitcher's Shaker House-Keeper*, a cookbook advertising

Canterbury Shaker medicines and other products distributed by Weeks and Potter of Boston, is printed about this time.

1886 The Canterbury Shakers register trademarks for their Shaker Compound of Wild Cherry Pectoral Syrup and the Sarsaparilla Lozenges.

1901 "The Dorothy" is registered as a trademark for cloaks made by the Canterbury Shakers.

1905 Elder Henry Blinn, one of the last great leaders of the Society, dies. Bertha Lindsay arrives at the village as a young orphan.

1912–1920 Several Canterbury Sisters nurse the remaining elderly members of the Union Village in Ohio. Three Ohio Sisters move to the Canterbury Society to live.

1916 The Church Family is the only active Family in the community. The membership consists of 2 Brothers; 47 Sisters; 1 male, aged 61 who remained 7 years; and 12 females less than 21 years old.

1917–1923 The Enfield, New Hampshire, Society closes. The remaining 13 members move to the Canterbury community.

1919 Arthur Bruce is the first Canterbury Shaker appointed as Lead Minister and serves with two Eldresses from New Lebanon. At Canterbury, the sarsaparilla kettles are removed from the Syrup Shop, and the building is remodelled for the Shakers' canning industry.

1920 The Canterbury Shakers sell their herds of Holstein and Guernsey cattle and begin buying dairy products.

1933 Irving Greenwood is appointed Lead Minister.

1934 The Canterbury Shaker school closes.

1937 The Canterbury Shakers begin buying their bread.

1947 The Mount Lebanon, New York, Shaker Society closes. The Lead Ministry moves to Hancock Shaker Village in Pittsfield, Massachusetts. The members of the Lead Ministry are

Frances Hall of Hancock and Josephine Wilson and Emma King of Canterbury.

1950 The membership in the Canterbury Shaker community consists of 16 Sisters between the ages of 46 and 83.

1957 The Lead Ministry moves to the Canterbury Society. The Lead Eldresses are Gertrude Soule from Sabbathday Lake and Ida Crook and Emma King from Canterbury.

1965 Marguerite Frost succeeds Ida Crook as Lead Minister. The Ministry vote to close the covenant membership of the Shaker Societies.

1967 Bertha Lindsay is selected as Eldress of the Canterbury community and as a member of the Lead Ministry.

1969 Shaker Village, Inc., a nonprofit corporation, is established to preserve and interpret the site of the Church Family.

1971 Charles Thompson serves as the first director of Shaker Village, Inc.

1972 Gertrude Soule, Lead Minister of the United Society, comes to Canterbury to live. The real estate of the Canterbury Shakers is conveyed to Shaker Village, Inc.

1987 Members of the Church Family are Eldress Bertha Lindsay, Eldress Gertrude Soule, and Sister Ethel Hudson.

CANTERBURY SHAKER VILLAGE, AS IT APPEARS TODAY

1. Trustees' Office (1830)
2. Meeting House (1792)
3. Ministry Shop (1848)
4. Children's House (1810)
5. Infirmary (1811)
6. Enfield House (1826)
7. Dwelling House (1793–1835)
8. Sisters' Shop (1817)
9. Carriage House (1825)
10. Carpenters' Shop (1806)
11. Brethrens' Shop (1824)
12. Creamery (1905)
13. Fire House (1908)
14. Power House (1910)
15. Garage (1923)
16. North Shop (1841)
17. Syrup Shop (1797)
18. Laundry (1795–1916)
19. Horse Barn (1819)
20. Schoolhouse (1823–1867)
21. Cart Shed (c. 1820)
22. Bee House (1837)
23. Arboretum (planted ca. 1850)
24. Barn (c. 1840) Foundation
25. Wood Shed
26. Herb Gardens
27. Site of Vegetable Garden

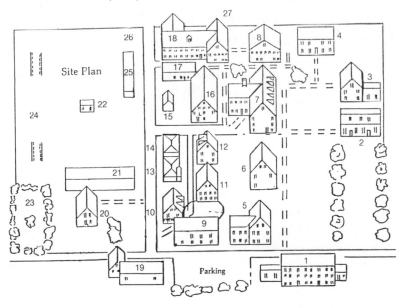

DIETARY TRADITIONS OF
THE CANTERBURY SHAKERS

It has been estimated that four thousand meals have been given away the present year [1846] at the North Family, to inquirers and young Believers not yet gathered to the Family.

> —Elder Henry Blinn, *"A Historical Record of the Society of Believers in Canterbury, New Hampshire,"* 1892

I recently had the privilege of sitting at Eldress Bertha's table for dinner. Bertha Lindsay and Gertrude Soule are the Lead Ministers of the United Society of Believers, and often entertain friends and scholars at the Trustees' Office, particularly during the winter months. In the summer and fall, when the village is open to the public, they spend most of their time greeting visitors and granting interviews. Knowing that the summer season was approaching, Bertha had arranged this special time for us to share, as she had done with other members of the Shaker Village, Inc., staff. I had been looking forward to the occasion, and Bertha, who takes pride in her ability to cook and prepare meals, was looking forward to it, too. As the meal slowly unfolded in front of me, I realized that her whole lifetime of cooking at Canterbury Shaker Village was virtually represented there at that table. She began the dinner with her Tomato Rice Soup, a dish she had learned to prepare from a former cooking companion sixty-five years ago. The vegetable dishes included parsnips, baked in a manner that had been passed down to her orally when she was a teenager. We also had pot roast, a favorite of Irving Greenwood, the last Canterbury Brother who lived at the village. Finally, for dessert, we had Lucy Shepard's Chocolate Steamed Pudding. The custard sauce served with it was made according to a recipe that had been jotted down by one of the cooks, probably in the 1930s. The meal would have pleased Eldress Josephine Wilson, a Sister who had lived and worked at the Trustees' Office for many years and had taught Bertha some of the fine points about presenting a dinner for company. The red tomato soup, golden parsnips, and green vegetables helped make the meal a pleasing mixture of colors, textures, and tastes.

The Shakers in their early years of settlement, however, would never have enjoyed such a repast. In the late eighteenth century, when that small group of farmers and artisans were gathering at the village, they had little opportunity to be concerned about diet, much less how colorfully a meal was prepared. The matters that received their immediate attention were the construction of the Meeting House and the Dwelling House, the organization of their internal structure, and supervising potential converts. The food that they managed to provide for themselves was simple indeed, if not monotonous. Elder Henry Blinn graphically described the hardships of those early days:

> *At times [the Canterbury Shakers] lived very sparingly. A dish of minced meat and potatoes, with a quantity of rye and Indian bread and a mug of old cider served for a meal. The farmers when they went with their teams to the woods, would often have their dinner prepared. This consisted at times of a large kettle of bean porridge. After [the porridge was] sufficiently cooked, one of the sled stakes was placed in the kettle and the mass allowed to freeze. It was now ready for transportation to the woods. The stake was returned to its place in the sled and the kettle bottom up, rode without harm. At noon the porridge was warmed and the dinner was received with Thanksgiving.[1]*

Porridge and hash appeared repeatedly at meals in the summer. Occasionally milk, butter, or cheese was added.

Bean porridge was served in the winter for breakfast and dinner. At noon "a liberal dish of meat and sauce" and pudding were typical fare.[2]

After the Meeting House and the Dwelling House were built, the Canterbury Shakers began, almost immediately, planting fruit trees,[3] constructing mills,[4] and gathering herds of farm animals as the next step in organizing themselves as a community. When the village entered the nineteenth century, the manufacture of cloth and the production of dairy products were major activities at the site. The trades helped supply clothing and food for the members and soon provided an income for the village. Blinn recorded that in 1801, the Canterbury Shakers processed 2,222 pounds of cheese and 942 pounds of butter. They also produced one hundred barrels of cider that year. Blinn's "Historical Record" indicates that by 1811 the Canterbury Shakers had sufficient numbers of cattle and swine to slaughter 5,835 pounds of beef and 5,616 pounds of pork. Applesauce appears to have been made for the first time at the community in 1815, and by 1824 the Shakers were selling medicinal herbs, which indicates that their gardens were well established.

As their prosperity increased, so did their consumption of food. From the late eighteenth century to about 1820, the Shakers were given considerable freedom when it came to their diet. One Canterbury Brother described their way of life as follows:

The people generally lived in a moderate, though comfortable and healthy style. They raised their own bread, meat, sauce, and sweetening, as well as all their articles of clothing from their own farms, and bought but very few necessaries whatever. Their common fare was puddings, meat, and sauce for dinner; and milk in the summer, and porridge with some kind of mince sauce for breakfast and supper in the winter. Sometimes a little butter or cheese for breakfast was set on with the porridge. Tea and coffee were generally used only once a week, the tea being of an ordinary quality; such as . . . sage balm and that growing on our plains called 'liberty tea.' . . . A very nutritious and wholesome diet.[5]

Even the consumption of liquor was not closely regulated during this period. The habit of imbibing was a European tradition that the colonists brought with them when they first settled this country, and fermentation was an acceptable and common method of preserving beverages. The Shakers followed the old ways.[6] Blinn noted that "cider wine" was an important part of the Canterbury Shakers' diet at that time.

Some of the old cider was distilled for the purpose of obtaining a weak quality of spirit, called "apple brandy," which was added to the new cider that was kept for drinking. The addition of the brandy arrested fermentation. . . . This was a much better article, if more brandy could make it better, and went by the name of 'Cider Wine.'[7]

In the late eighteenth and early nineteenth centuries, however, people of the "World," and soon the Shakers as well, began to look at the consumption of cider and "spirits" with some concern. The first written regulations the Lead Ministry imposed on the Shaker Societies were issued in 1821 in the Millenial Laws, but even in that case the Shakers were given a lot of leeway.[8] The Laws stated that members were not allowed to indulge in cider or "distilled spirits" on Sunday. If a Shaker was involved in "fatiguing chores" on that day, he or she was then permitted to drink but only between breakfast and noon. No one was allowed to partake in "ardent spirits" out in the "World." If a person was ill, he or she was allowed to "get a little wine." The Laws were also lenient when it came to the consumption of food. It was written that the Shakers were not allowed to eat cucumbers unless the fruits were seasoned with salt or pepper. The Shakers were also told that they were permitted to eat raw fruit and nuts only between breakfast and six o'clock in the afternoon. A person who had to have a different diet was allowed to "freely go to the cooks" and ask to have the food specially prepared. The Lead Ministry's attitude toward diet is probably best summarized by this statement in the Millennial Laws: "But the order for all Believers is to be free & to ask for just what they need and that which is not worth asking for is not worth having."[9]

Apparently, the Shakers did not follow even these mild stipulations too closely. Blinn noted:

> *It had been a universal custom for all who chose to do so, to take a glass of spirits every morning before breakfast, as an appetiser, and then more or less through the day as circumstances favored.*[10]

The New Lebanon Society continued to apply some pressure on the Shakers with regard to their use of alcoholic beverages. In 1828 the New Lebanon physicians distributed copies of a letter entitled, "The Death of Old Alcohol," and "appropriate ceremonies, in funeral form, were held in every Society." While the rituals focused on "alcoholic drams," the Shakers also restricted their consumption of cider somewhat. The portions were reduced to one fourth of a pint of cider at breakfast and one-half of a pint at dinner for each Brother; each Sister was allowed one third of that amount. In addition to those allotments, each Brother was still permitted one quart of cider during the day.[11] Many of the apple trees were subsequently cut down, and some of the orchard land was converted into a garden. From 1837 to 1847 neither Henry Blinn nor John Whitcher kept an account of the harvesting of apples.

By the 1840s the temperance movement in the "World" had expanded to include stiffer restrictions on solid food as well. Some of the Shakers had also become increasingly concerned about the quantities of meat that were being consumed at every meal.

> *The Believers had lived plainly as a whole, but were consumers of a great deal of beef and swine's flesh. The younger classes were unable to digest so much of the animal fats . . .* [12]

Having talked with Brother Garrett Lawrence (1794–1839), a doctor at New Lebanon, Thomas Corbett (1780–1857), the physician at the Canterbury Society, recommended that members adhere to the advice of Sylvester Graham, a dietician of the "World." The Graham diet involved abstaining from condiments, stimulants, meat, and animal fats. The only beverage allowed was water. The system was recommended by the Shakers for young Believers in particular, to benefit them physically and mentally. To Blinn, the new regimen was a "radical change" for the Canterbury Shakers, many of whom were eating "meat and butter, more or less, three times a day, and [drinking] tea and coffee . . . "[13] In 1836, the New Hampshire Ministry reported optimistically:

> . . . *this work of temperance progresses; as we understand there are between 30 and 40 in the Church who do not drink Tea, Coffee, nor Chorkolate, but have become waterites. Graham bread and the like seem to be preferred by many . . .* [14]

But the Ministry spoke too soon. The diet was not enthusiastically embraced by either the young Believers or the cooks, and the old habits returned in about a year.[15] In 1841 the Canterbury Society received an "inspirational" message from the Lead Ministry reinforcing the old ban. Again the restriction was focused on the youthful members, and the Shakers were given some freedom regarding compliance. All members younger than sixty were requested to abstain from eating pork and drinking tea and coffee. Blinn recorded that they were encouraged to drink "Meadow Sweet and Liberty Tea" (*Seanothus Americanus*, a plant that grew in Concord) and other home-grown concoctions as substitutes for imported tea. In place of coffee, the Canterbury Shakers were told to use "barley, peas, and roasted carrots and the root of 'Avens,' *Geum rivale* [a herb that grew near the village ponds]." Persons older than sixty years were allowed to choose whether or not to follow the new orders. Those who had the freedom to choose did not agree among themselves. At the time the restriction was issued, there were forty-two members living at the Church Family who were older than sixty years. Twenty-nine of those members volunteered to comply, whereas five Brothers and eight Sisters did not.[16]

The Canterbury Shakers continued to raise swine,

nonetheless. From about 1811 to 1848, nearly six thousand pounds of pork were slaughtered each year. A portion of the meat was sold, but pork remained a part of the Shakers' habitual nourishment for some of the residents at least.

In 1848, another message was issued from New Lebanon, again emphasizing the prohibition on the sale and consumption of pork. After August 30 of that year, pork was no longer placed on the table at Canterbury. The Trustees sold what they had on hand, except for what was served the hired men. According to Blinn, "inspirational messages" were received from Mother Ann and other leaders of the past, urging Believers to refrain from indulging not only in pork, but also tea, coffee, liquor, cider, and tobacco. For ten years, the Shakers refrained from eating pork and selling swine. Blinn reported that "if the cooks were so fortunate as to obtain a suitable article for the mince pies they felt quite satisfied." Tea and coffee were given to members only by special request, and "the drinking of drams . . . passed away."[17]

The Canterbury Shakers continued to flavor their food liberally, however. From about 1847 to 1854, they sold four herbs for culinary purposes: sage, summer savory, thyme, and sweet majoram.[18] They also sold rose water from 1849 to about 1865. Maple sugar and honey were used frequently to sweeten food. Molasses was used in making beer and medicine, and maple sugar was made into "sweet cake." Blinn reported that "oatmeal found its place every morning at the breakfast table, and was relished by many with its brimming of cream and sugar."[19]

In general, the second half of the nineteenth century saw a relaxation of the earlier injunctions. Canterbury Shaker cooks collected the best recipes from the "World" and adapted them for their own use.[20] In 1850 cider made its way back to the table again. Coffee and imported tea were reintroduced in 1861.[21] The following year the Shakers were raising swine once more, although, interestingly enough, the argument for having them return was not for dietary reasons but for "profits." From 1862 to 1871, the animals were "generally" sold live and were slaughtered off the site. It is also probable that after 1871, the Canterbury Shakers began to butcher swine again at the community.

About 1882 *Mary Whitcher's Shaker House-Keeper*, a cook-book, was printed for use by the "World." It contained advertisements and testimonials lauding the merits of the Canterbury Shakers' sarsaparilla syrup and other medicines distributed by Weeks and Potter, wholesale agents in Boston. The book was probably produced to aid in the sale of these medicines. It is also possible that the recipes were provided by Weeks and Potter and that the Canterbury Shakers lent the name of one of their Trustees as an endorsement. It is worth examining the recipes, however, because they may give some idea as to what kinds of food the Shakers felt they should publicly support. In her introduction, Whitcher noted: "The Shakers recognize the fact that good food, properly cooked and well digested, is the basis of sound health." Dishes, she added, should be "savory" as well as "economical." Traditional, basic fare such as roast leg of mutton, boiled dinner, baked potatoes, and boiled rice were mentioned along with more elegant offerings such as wine jelly and turbot à la crème. The book included several recipes for meat dishes and desserts (mainly cakes and puddings), a small number of seafood recipes, and few recipes for vegetables. A typical dinner, according to the menus provided, consisted of soup, a red meat dish, potatoes, and pudding. Salt, pepper, and sugar were frequently added to foods. Mace and allspice were required occasionally; nutmeg was often added to desserts; and ginger and molasses were used in breads and cakes. Flavorings included extracts of lemon, almond, and vanilla, as well as currants, raisins, citron, celery, and onion juice. Parsley, mustard, sage, and cayenne were used to accent main meat dishes. Recipes for ham, stews, sauces, and pickles called for cloves. Some of the recipes were labelled "Shaker," although the majority seem to have been taken from newspaper clippings from across the country. The Shaker Fish and Egg dish, for example, came from the *Chicago Times*.

At the turn of the century, the Canterbury Shaker cooks continued to follow some of the habits of the Sisters who preceded them. Several varieties of foods were served at the table. The main meal consisted of soup (occasionally), one or two types of meat, bread, several kinds of vegetables, and at least one kind of dessert, often pie. Applesauce was served three times a day. Soups, steak, and pies were more often prepared for company and hired help than they were for the Sisters at the Dwelling House. Generally, the food was slightly higher in quality at the Trustees' Office, where the Shakers represented themselves to the "World." Red meat and butter were frequently part of the diet until the 1940s or 1950s. About that time, the Shakers' physician began to regulate the Sisters' intake of animal fats as well as salt. Cooks were encouraged to experiment with dishes and make them look festive. The Sisters rarely owned their own cookbooks, but they did use those that were stored at the Dwelling House. As did their Sisters of the nineteenth century, the cooks and bakers kept scrapbooks in which they collected favorite recipes from newspapers and magazines. Today, the Shaker culinary tradition has come full circle, with Eldress Bertha trying out recipes found in Shaker cookbooks compiled by culinary experts today and adapting them for her own use at the village.

COOKING AND BAKING AT CANTERBURY SHAKER VILLAGE IN THE TWENTIETH CENTURY

"April Fool's Day. Family came down to breakfast with no dishes or food on tables. After enjoying the joke, [the cooks brought in] six trays, one for each table, using as few dishes as possible."

—Jessie Evans,
diary entry, May 15, 1905

The community members had to organize their cooking in order to feed the large numbers of Believers, potential converts, visitors, and hired help. Originally, each of the four Families had its own kitchen and dining room. By 1916 the only active Family at the village was the Church Family with about sixty members to feed. The Dwelling House, built in 1793, provided a dining hall, a kitchen, and a bakery as well as a private room for the Ministry to have their meals. (The latter was used only for special occasions in the twentieth century, however.) The dining room had about seven tables, and two seatings were provided. Three tables were used at the second seating for children and the elderly. A few of the members ate at the Trustees' Office, built in 1831, across the road from the rest of the Church Family. The building had a post office from 1848 to 1939 and was the place where the Shakers shipped goods to and received them from the "World." The Shakers constructed a kitchen and two dining rooms there, one for hired men and one for more genteel company. In 1880 they added the south kitchen where the Sisters made beer and switchel for the workers in the field.

Kitchens and dining rooms were remodelled as the membership changed; the duties evolved, and technology improved. The kitchens were large and had built-in cupboards designed for many uses. A few of the storage units had double bread boards that could be pulled out when needed, enabling two Sisters to work together. Sometimes a kitchen was equipped with more than one stove. In 1909, according to Brother Irving Greenwood, the Shakers provided the Dwelling House kitchen with two new ranges (a New Eldorado and a Franconia #10) and a broiler from the Mirandi Proctor Company of Boston. Electrical wiring was installed the following year. In 1926 the Shakers bought a used KitchenAid. The next year they purchased a second-hand meat slicer and installed a Frigidaire in the pantry. In 1929 they added Sunbeam heaters. In 1937 a new range was purchased, apparently to replace the other stoves.

The Office kitchen was remodelled extensively in 1913. Walls were torn down to enlarge the room, and new shelving and two iron sinks were added. Every few years, a range was brought in to replace one that was apparently unsatisfactory. Josephine Wilson reported in her diary that in 1920 they moved a stove that had come from the Dwelling House at the Enfield, New Hampshire Shaker, community to the Canterbury Office kitchen. About eight months later, they replaced that stove with another that had also come from Enfield. In 1939, to relieve the Office cooks, the Shakers provided a separate kitchen for the hired hands. They gave the men the Office stove and supplied the cooks with a new range. Since 1946 Bertha has purchased at least three new electric stoves for that space. Around 1966 she modernized the kitchen again with the addition of a stainless steel double sink unit.

The spaces were designed to accommodate groups of two or three cooks who worked together. The teams were selected by an Eldress. Traditionally, the work was rotated about once a month. In the twentieth century, depending on the health of the Sisters and other activities within the community, the women worked about four weeks in the kitchen and eight weeks on a craft industry (making sweaters, cloaks, and other items for sale). The rotation system benefited the Sisters for several reasons. It allowed them to have new work partners periodically, an important consideration since the more capable women were sometimes paired with those who needed supervision. The routine also gave the apprentices a chance to prove their abilities in several areas. The Sisters learned different tasks and were thus able to "fill in" when a Shaker was sick or had another job to do. (Bertha frequently substituted in the kitchen when other Sisters had to sell goods off the site.) The work routine for the cooks and bakers required that the Sisters rise at four-thirty in the morning. The duty, including the cleaning that followed the meal, lasted until about two o'clock in the afternoon. At that point, the cooks and bakers were allowed some leisure time until the preparation of the supper began.

The Dwelling House team consisted of a "head cook," who planned the meals and cooked the meats; a "second cook," who washed and cooked the vegetables; and a "third cook," or "messer." The messer had her own work space and fixed special dishes for the elderly or sick members and for the Ministry. Two Sisters worked in the bakery and made bread, pies, and pastries for the entire community.

The Office team had a similar routine. Work was divided among the head cook, who planned the meals and cooked the meats and vegetables, a second cook, who made the desserts, and a young resident, who set the tables and cleaned the dining areas. Unless the cooks had invited the dinner guests, they ate in the kitchen with the two female Trustees. In the summer months, when the heated oven made the kitchen uncomfortable, the cooks and Trustees ate in the smaller south kitchen.

The Canterbury Sisters learned to cook in a manner that is similar to an apprentice system. The young ones began to learn about the kitchen duties by cleaning the spaces and cooking simple dishes. After they had mastered those tasks, they were given a more challenging job. The girls learned by watching and imitating their older Sisters. By the time a young woman was permitted to make a cake or pie, she was well trained and required no supervision.

—*M.R.B.*

Plate 3.   Bertha Lindsay, aged twelve, 1909. *Kimball Studios, Concord, New Hampshire.*

INTRODUCTION [1]

*"Be faithful to keep the gospel. Be neat and industrious.
Have everything in your house arranged in order and in
neatness. Prepare your food in that manner that those who
partake of it may bless you with thankful hearts. Keep a
strict watch over the words you speak, that you may not
treat others unkindly nor cast on them unpleasant reflec-
tions. Let your words be few and seasoned with grace."*

> —Mother Ann Lee, as quoted in *The Life and Gos-
> pel Experience of Mother Ann Lee*, by Elder Henry
> Blinn, published by the Shakers, East Canter-
> bury, N.H. (1883).

While the Shakers are particularly famous for beautiful
and simple furniture, equal attention should be given to our
cooking. There is something to the axiom that cooks are
born, not made. Although I believe that all people can learn
to cook and prepare a good meal, natural ability allows a
person to give extra attention to whatever is made. Indeed,
cooking is an art just as much as painting a picture or making
a piece of furniture. For if a meal is prepared with fine
produce, the natural cook knows how to give it the special
touch, not only making it eye-appealing, but also delicious.

I might say that this talent of mine was inherited from my
mother, a cook of renown in the town where she lived.[2]
However, I owe my success in this field to the kind Sisters
with whom I have lived for eighty years. I came to
Canterbury Shaker Village when I was seven, receiving all my
education under the tutelage of patient, loving Sisters. At that

age, the world of make-believe was still a playtime joy. I can remember, as anyone raised in the country may recollect, making all conceivable dishes of mud—mud-pies decorated with milkweed down for whipped cream were a specialty. Menus were a delight to plan; the supply unlimited. Being quite imaginative, I would invite my playmates to a sumptuous meal.

Many of the Shaker women were very good cooks. The Shakers felt that teaching a little girl of ten or eleven to cook potatoes would be valuable for her, as that is the age in which she can learn easily. The little girls were first taught the different ways of cooking potatoes so that by the time they were thirteen, they had mastered the art and were moved on to some other task, like making pies or helping in the bake room. So, in our kitchen department there were three Sisters and a fourth member who was a little girl between ten and fifteen years of age. There was the head cook, second cook, and a "messer" who fixed the trays of food for the older people who either needed special dishes or who could not come to the dining room to eat. The young member did whatever was needed and took care of the potatoes.

I started cooking the potatoes under the teaching of Sister Rebecca Hathaway, who was an excellent cook. We were taught from the beginning to do our work as perfectly as possible, following the advice of our Founder Mother Ann Lee to prepare the meals so that those who partook could do so with grateful hearts. At the age of thirteen, I was taught to make the pies. I worked with several Sisters in the bake room: Hope Vickery, Gertna Curtis, Helena Sarle, and Lena Crook, all of whom were excellent bread makers. Under their tutelage, I was able to learn to make the bread, and, by the time I was eighteen, assume the responsibility myself, which I was very fond of doing. By the time I was twenty, I was removed from the bake room, because Sister Josephine Wilson wanted me at the Office kitchen. As head cook there, I planned the meals, prepared the meats, and did the cooking for the company, the Office Sisters, and the hired help. At that time, we had about fifteen men working for us, because our Brothers had grown fewer in number and were less able to do the work that was left. During the summer I first started working there, the Shakers hired twenty-five men for painting some of the buildings and for haying. It was really quite an experience for me to cook for so many people.

The Shakers rotated their work, so we took turns of four weeks apiece to do one duty, and then we would change and other Sisters would come in and take four weeks to do that work. Many times, when Sisters Frieda Weeks and Eunice Clarke were out selling Shaker articles, I would be in the Office kitchen eight weeks at a time because we would have to fill in for those who went out to sell, as that was an important feature of our livelihood.[3]

We had very fine fresh vegetables and fruits right from our own gardens and trees. Our meals were not considered "gourmet," but plain country cooking. Nourishing, healthy meals were always served. Sister Josephine was very particular as to how a table looked, not only the table settings, but also the food. She taught us early to have color in the meal, to make it eye-appealing.

In any Shaker kitchen now, I am sure you will find cookbooks of many different varieties: Mennonite, French, All-American, Italian, and German. Looking through my cookbooks now, you will also find two books with pasted-in recipes.[4] When I first started cooking, I was interested in cutting out different recipes that appealed to me from the *Ladies' Home Journal, Woman's Day, Family Circle,* and *Better Homes and Gardens.* It has been my privilege to cook many of these very fine recipes, the Shakers being very willing to try anything that would be nice to put onto the table.

In this little book the recipes come from many sources, as you will see. They are my favorites that I have made to please our Family. I have tried to make the recipes available to average homes. Of course, with freezers so popular today, there are many things that can be preserved for later use. So, if the dish is too much for a family to eat at one time, there's always the freezer to help at a time of emergency.

Have some pleasant memories of yesteryear and of today, and good eating!

— *Eldress Bertha Lindsay*

Plate 4.   Independence Day dinner at the Cow Barn, July 4, 1924.
Shaker Archives, 11–P160, SVI.

In 1924, to celebrate Independence Day, the Shakers held a
dinner in their vacant Cow Barn. They invited their friends the
Parkhursts and Shaws as guests and served the food "cafeteria
style." Tables were arranged in a line on the "feeding floor," and
diners helped themselves to dishes of food placed nearby before
they sat down together for the meal. Cooks and bakers were Cora
Helena Sarle, Mildred Wells, Evelyn Polsey, and Miriam Wall. The
dinner consisted of clam chowder, vegetable soup, steamed clams,
clam cakes, lobsters, quahogs, vegetable salad, peas, two kinds of
pies, and watermelon, and was judged a "success." Supper followed later "on the lawn," and the Shakers ended the day with a
"sing" in the Meeting House.

Soups and Stews[1]

"Mr. and Mrs. McKee out here to dinner. Bertha and Mildred in kitchen. Have clam chowder."

—Josephine E. Wilson,
diary entry, February 17, 1938

*W*hat could be more desirable on a cold winter day than a nice bowl of hot soup as a starter or as a main dish? We did not have soups with every dinner, but Sisters Josephine Wilson and Blanche Gardner taught me how to make them for the company in the Trustees' Office.

It was about this time that the Sisters learned how to make clam chowder the Rhode Island way, and, of course, that is the New England way, as the New York people like tomato in theirs. We made our clam chowder in the big kettle in the kitchen. We had it two-thirds full and set a fire beneath it. In 1924, Mr. Henry Hathaway, father of Sister Rebecca Hathaway, came on a visit from Providence, Rhode Island, bringing friends, the Tuckers. They wanted very much to have a clambake for the village members, and the Barn seemed a very fitting place to hold it for everyone wanted to join. In 1920, the Shaker herd of Guernseys and Holsteins was sold. The Cow Barn at that time was house cleaned and made presentable for anything we wanted. So, for our clambake, tables were set the full length of the Barn, and

chairs were obtained. Mr. Hathaway and Mr. Tucker saw to
the digging of the pit where the clams were to be steamed
and the corn roasted. The Sisters had very little to do except
provide the watermelon and whatever else that was needed.
But the whole Family joined in the partaking of this delicious
meal. (See plate 7.)

This New England Clam Chowder is a favorite of
Eldress Gertrude.

New England Clam Chowder

1–2 onions, chopped
2 tablespoons margarine or
  2" square of salt pork
3 cups clam juice
2 potatoes, medium, cubed

1 pint shell clams, minced
  (or 7-ounce can minced
  clams)
2 cups milk
A few soda crackers
Salt and pepper

Sauté an onion or two in margarine. (I don't use salt
pork anymore. But if you use salt pork, sauté until well
done.) Add clam juice and potatoes and cook until
potatoes are almost soft. Add clams. Clams don't
require much cooking and will get hard if cooked too
long. Add milk and heat slowly. We were taught to put
in milk, about a pint, a few soda crackers, broken up,
not too fine. That is what thickens it a little. Add salt and
pepper to taste.

Serves 6   —Quoted to the editor, 1986

∽

At one point in my cooking, I worked with Mildred
Wells who had a grandmother living in Hungary. She
was privileged to visit her grandmother when younger
and learned many Hungarian dishes from her, among
them: Hungarian Goulash, Cabbage Stuffed Leaves,
Apple Strudel, and this delicious Rice Tomato Soup.

Rice Tomato Soup

1½ quarts tomatoes, strained	½ tablespoon flour
Pinch baking soda	¼ cup sugar
⅔ cup rice, cooked	Salt and pepper, to taste
1 cup soured cream	

To strain tomatoes, put through a food mill. Add baking soda to tomatoes. Combine tomatoes and rice. Heat to boiling point. Add flour and sugar to soured cream and add to tomatoes. Cook gently while stirring constantly. Serve.

Serves 4–6

—The Canterbury Shakers, *Shaker Tested Recipes,* Canterbury, New Hampshire, 1965

Cream of Squash Soup

4 cups thin white sauce (see page 61.)	1 teaspoon orange peel, grated
½ cup winter squash, cooked, drained	Whipped cream
⅛ teaspoon ground ginger	Paprika

To the hot, well-seasoned white sauce, add the squash, ginger, and orange peel. Beat until thoroughly blended. To serve, heat and top with a spoonful of whipped cream and a dash of paprika.

Serves 6

—*Pictorial Review Standard Cookbook*

I am not sure whether the early Shakers found mushrooms appealing in their meals, but the modern Shakers have certainly used them many times. Here, in

New England, we have a mushroom called the
"puffball," which is excellent not only for frying, but
also for making into delicious Cream of Mushroom
Soup.

Cream of Mushroom Soup

2 tablespoons butter
1 8-ounce can mushrooms
(or 1 cup fresh
mushrooms)
1 tablespoon flour
1 cup juice from canned
mushrooms (or 1 cup
chicken broth)

1 cup milk
¼ cup light cream
1 egg yolk
Salt to taste
2 tablespoons parsley,
chopped
Dash paprika

Melt butter in 2-quart saucepan. Add drained and
chopped mushrooms. Sauté for 10 minutes. Add flour
and juice or stock and cook, covered, for 20 minutes on
low heat. Add milk, cream, and egg yolk. Season with
salt. Heat well and serve garnished with parsley and
paprika.

Serves 4   —Bertha Lindsay's "Geography"

The lentil is an ancient vegetable, spoken of in the
Bible. Today, the Lentil Soup is a delicious starter for
any meal.

Lentil Soup

1 pound lentils
2 cups chicken broth
½ teaspoon salt

¼ teaspoon pepper
Dash oregano
½ teaspoon butter

Wash and rinse lentils thoroughly, checking for stones
or sand. Cover lentils with cold water and bring to boil.
Reduce heat and cook until soft, about 2 hours. Add

chicken broth, salt, pepper, and oregano. Blend ingredients. Just before serving, heat and top with butter.

Serves 4-6   —Quoted to the editor, 1985

The Shakers had beautiful vegetable gardens. Elder Arthur Bruce was very proud of his vegetable garden[2] and the beautiful straight rows in it. We planted a variety of vegetables and lots of every kind to provide not only for the table but also for friends and for the needy. The Vegetable Soup was a special favorite among the early Shakers.

Shaker Vegetable Soup

1 quart boiling water	*1 stalk celery, sliced*
2 potatoes, medium, diced	*2 tablespoons barley*
1 carrot, sliced	*¾ cup light cream*
1 turnip, small, diced	*1 teaspoon butter*

To boiling water, add vegetables and barley. Cook until done. Season and add cream and butter. Ten minutes before serving, make batter (see below). While soup is still boiling, pour batter into it slowly. It will float around on top and will have the taste of vermicelli.

Batter

1 egg   *1 cup milk*   *Flour*

Mix egg and milk together and add flour until the mixture drops off a spoon easily.

Serves 6   —*Shaker Tested Recipes*

Lamb stew serves as a nice main dish. Serve it with the Rice Pineapple Dainty or the Fruit Rice Bavarian Pudding for dessert. (See page 80.)

Lamb Stew

2 cups cubed lamb, for stewing
2 onions, medium, chopped
1 tablespoon butter
4–5 carrots, cut up into bite-size chunks

4–5 potatoes, cut similarly
2 tablespoons barley
Chicken or beef broth (optional)

Plate 5. Clambake, between the Cow Barn (background) and the Syrup Shop, July 9, 1924. *Shaker Archives, 11–P157, SVI.*

In the twentieth century, the Canterbury Shakers held many "shore dinners." Friends and relatives brought them varieties of seafood, and the Shakers provided the rest of the ingredients of the meal. Pictured here may be Henry Hathaway, father of Sister Rebecca. On July 9, he and his friends left Providence, Rhode Island at four o'clock in the morning, bringing fresh lobsters and clams. They steamed the clams outside, and the dinner was held at one o'clock in the renovated barn.

Cover fresh lamb with water and stew for 1 hour. (Leftover lamb may be used but does not need to be boiled for more than ½ hour.) Cool. Remove fat. Sauté onions in butter until transparent. Add carrots and potatoes and cook for about 5 minutes. Add this mixture to the lamb and broth. If broth is inadequate, supplement with chicken or beef broth. Stew for 2 hours. If a thick stew is desired, add barley in last hour of cooking.

Serves 4–6 —Quoted to the editor, 1985

Plate 6.   Brother Irving Greenwood, and friend Dewey, probably at the Trustees' Office, February, 1923. *Shaker Archives, 1–PN168, SVI.*

Meats, Poultry and Fish[1]

"Dorothea Cochran and Jane Crooker go to Lowell [Massachusetts] to cook fish-egg for a dinner, by ex-Mayor Stoot's request."

—Anonymous, *"Church Record II,"* May 1, 1889

Shaker homes were well organized. The kitchen facilities, like other departments, were cared for by a Deaconess and a Deacon. The Deaconess took care of all the canned provisions and utensils. The Deacon took care of the meats and garden produce. Chickens, dairy cattle, pigs and sheep were once raised at the village to help provide for the meals.

Our ponds were always stocked in the spring with little fingerlings of pickerel, horned pout and perch. Catching our fish in the spring was a particularly fun time, because we had a stove at the Ice Mill Pond where we would cook our food, and we made a regular picnic out of it. There was a little railroad track coming from the Wood Mill, out as far as at least one section of the pond.[2] And so we would carry all the things out to our stove in the little car that ran on the tracks. And I'll tell you, baking powder biscuits never tasted so good as when baked on top of that old stove. We had ample food for our picnic supper with the lovely fried fish, biscuits, and whatever we'd want to take down besides. (See plates 6–8.)

It was a custom to have our dinner at noon, like all country people did. It would consist of beef, lamb, fish, or chicken with a potato of some sort, two vegetables, and a dessert of some kind, usually a piece of pie or pudding. The meals were simple, but nourishing. A motto of the Shakers was to "Shaker your plate," meaning people could take as much as they wanted, but they had to eat entirely what they put on their plate and not leave any for waste.

The Shakers always provided for guests who desired a hot dinner. Back in the 1800s, a simple meal was served. It consisted of the Shaker Fish and Egg; a nice, fresh vegetable; fresh, home-baked bread; and the baked, or boiled, apple. About one hundred years ago, Mary Whitcher, Canterbury Trustee, compiled a few recipes in the *Shaker House-Keeper,* a little book that was well sought after in her day. In it, she included the Shaker Fish and Egg.

Mary used a double boiler for this recipe, but I don't.

Shaker Fish and Egg

1 generous cup salted, dried
*   codfish, shredded (not fresh*
*   or frozen)*
2 cups light cream

1 tablespoon butter
3 potatoes, medium, boiled,
*   sliced*
6 eggs, hard-boiled, sliced
½ teaspoon pepper

Soak the codfish in cold water 2–3 hours or overnight. Then drain, rinse and soak again in fresh water while preparing this dish. Scald the cream; add butter. In a buttered baking dish, place a layer of potatoes, sprinkle a layer of codfish, then place a layer of eggs. Repeat and add seasonings. Cover with cream. Simmer in a slow oven, 300 degrees, for ten minutes. Garnish with sliced or minced hard-boiled eggs.

Serves 6   —Mary Whitcher, *Shaker House-Keeper*

Fried Chicken Supreme

1 3-pound chicken	*¾ cup water*
1 egg	*1 teaspoon salt*
1 tablespoon water	*⅛ teaspoon pepper*
1 cup fine crumbs	*1 cup light cream*
4 tablespoons fat	

Cut the chicken into serving pieces. Dip in egg that has been slightly beaten with water, then in crumbs. Brown on all sides in fat. Add water and seasonings. Simmer about 1 hour, or until tender. Add cream, cover, and cook gently about 15 minutes longer.

Serves 4

—Shaker Tested Recipes

The following is a good way to use leftover meat.

Savory Meat

1 pound meat, ground	*Salt and pepper, to taste*
1 egg, beaten	*1 scant teaspoon sage*

Add egg and seasonings to meat. Moisten with water. [The reader may want to substitute broth or a vegetable liquid for the water.] Put in a small loaf pan and bake 35–40 minutes at 325 degrees until brown.

Serves 2–4

—Gourmet's Delight

When I worked at the Office kitchen, I used to cook a pot roast that was a favorite of Brother Irving. In those days, he slept in that building, and when a pot roast was cooked, he'd go downstairs at night and take off with some of the best part. The next morning he would laugh and tell me the kitchen cat ate it.

Brother Irving Greenwood's Pot Roast

shortening   Worcestershire sauce
1 4-pound beef roast   1 onion, medium
Flour   Salt and pepper, to taste
Tenderizer (optional)   Water

The following method of cooking a roast tenderizes the
meat. Select a tough cut, such as a beef round or
shoulder. Put a little shortening in a frying pan. Roll the
meat in a little flour and completely cover it to help it
get brown. Add a tenderizer (made from papaya) if
preferred. Sprinkle the tenderizer on the meat and fork
it in to make sure it gets inside the roast. Put the floured
roast in the heated fry pan and keep turning the meat
until it is brown all over. Add other ingredients. Keep
adding just enough water to keep the roast simmering
for about 3 hours. When the roast is done, there will be
about a pint of nice, dark, rich, well-seasoned gravy.
Thicken the gravy and serve separately with the roast
and baked potatoes.

Serves 5–6
                              —Quoted to the editor, 1986

Veal with Sour Cream

4–6 veal chops   3 tablespoons butter
Salt and pepper   1 cup sour cream
Flour   1 egg yolk, beaten

Bone and cut chops short. Season with salt and pepper.
Dip in flour. Melt butter in fry pan. Add chops and fry
slowly, turning to brown evenly. Place in a baking dish,
pour the cream over (save a little for later), and bake

slowly for about 20 minutes. Remove to a hot platter. Slowly pour the sauce from the pan over the yolk mixed with a little cream. Serve on chops.

Serves 4–6

—*Shaker Tested Recipes*

Shaker Baked Fish

1 4–6 pound fish, whole	*Dash paprika*
5 soda crackers, crushed	*1 tablespoon parsley*
1 tablespoon butter	*Fish broth*
1 teaspoon salt	*Salt pork strips*
1 teaspoon thyme, minced	*Flour*

Scrape fish and wash clean. Season with salt. To make broth, simmer head and tail in enough water to cover. Make a dressing with crackers, butter, salt, herbs, and enough broth to make it very moist. Stuff fish with this preparation and fasten with a skewer. Cut slits in the fish and put pork into them. Dredge with flour and place in a buttered baking dish. Bake 1 hour, in a 300 degree oven, basting often. Surround with tomato sauce (see page 61).

Serves 4–6

—Mary Whitcher, *Shaker House-Keeper*

Stuffing

The Shakers raised many herbs in the early days. When I first came to Canterbury, the Shakers were still growing some herbs for the kitchen use. At the top of the garden, just over the fence by the Laundry, Sister Rebecca raised sage which she ground and sold in the gift shop. The sale of powdered sage was quite a business in those days; we had a little machine that would grind it up very fine. Later, Brother Irving fixed the machine with a belt so that it could be run electrically, and this helped Rebecca a great deal. She took care of the garden right up to the year that she passed away. We used sage in our stuffing for chicken and turkey, as we preferred this to many other herbs.

Bread Stuffing

3 cups stale bread cubes
2 tablespoons onion, chopped
¼ cup fat, melted
1 cup celery, etc. (see below)
½ cup stock or milk

Salt, pepper, paprika, sage,
*   or poultry seasoning to*
*   taste*
Parsley, to taste (optional)

Cut bread into ⅜″ cubes. (Cubes give lightness to the stuffing, since they do not pack into a soggy mess as crumbs do. To give color, use the crust or brown a third of the cubes in the oven or in the fat used in the stuffing. Leftover toast may be used instead of bread.) Cook onion in the fat until lightly browned and add to the bread. Add an ingredient to give individuality to the stuffing. It may be cooked, chopped celery, sautéed mushrooms, chopped olives, cooked giblets, hard-cooked eggs, or oysters cooked in milk, or a combination of two or more of these ingredients. Add liquid to moisten. The exact amount will depend on the dryness of the bread. It is best to allow the mixture to stand for half an hour or longer, so that the bread will have a chance to absorb the liquid and be moistened throughout. Add seasonings to taste.

—Pictorial Review Standard Cookbook

Plate 7. Canterbury Shakers and friends cook on the wood stove at the Ice Mill Pond, c. 1924. *Shaker Archives, 1–PN81, SVI.*

We had only a few nut trees around the village.[3] For a while, we harvested many chestnuts, which we roasted or boiled. They were good for just plain eating, but we also made them into a delicious stuffing.

Chestnut Stuffing

3 cups chestnut purée
1 cup bread crumbs, soft
½ cup butter or margarine,
    melted
1 tablespoon parsley, chopped

1 tablespoon onion, grated
½ teaspoon salt
⅛ teaspoon pepper
½ cup cream

To prepare purée, boil a quart of large French chestnuts until tender. Remove shells and skins and rub through a sieve. Add the bread crumbs, butter, and seasonings to the purée. Moisten with cream and mix lightly. Use with chicken or turkey.

Serves 5   —*Pictorial Review Standard Cookbook*

Oyster Stuffing

¼ cup milk
½ cup butter or margarine,
    melted
3 cups bread crumbs, soft

1 pint oysters, chopped
2½ teaspoons salt
½ teaspoon pepper

Pour milk and butter over crumbs. Add oysters and seasonings.

Serves 5   —*Pictorial Review Standard Cookbook*

Plate 8. Canterbury Shaker Sisters at dinner at the Ice Mill Pond, c. 1920. Bertha Lindsay *(far left)*, Rebecca Hathaway *(second from right)*, Leona Merrill Rowell *(standing)*. *Shaker Archives, 15–P72, SVI.*

The Sisters are wearing their "dust caps" and are probably taking a break from cleaning the mills. Bertha remembers that the Sisters cleaned the mills each year: " . . . we donned our oldest clothes, and little groups of Sisters with the young people were sent to clean the mills . . . This meant that the windows all had to be washed so they were bright and clean, the cobwebs brushed down, and the floors swept neatly so that everything was in apple pie order to commence another year. [After] the work, of course, we had the fun of having a picnic dinner around the north end of the Ice Mill Pond. It was an open clearing with beautiful big maple trees. Here, we had a stove where we could cook our dinner, and it was usually Sister Helena and Rebecca that got the dinner for us."

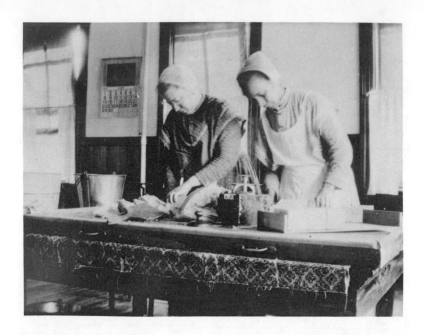

Plate 9.   Working in the Creamery, June, 1919. Edith Green *(right)*.
Shaker Archives, 12–P160, SVI.

The processing of cheese and butter was one of the most successful businesses at Canterbury and had one of the longest histories at the village, dating back to at least 1801. For about seventy-five years, the Canterbury Shakers made, on the average, two thousand pounds of butter and three thousand pounds of cheese annually. In 1905 the operation moved to the Creamery which was built by contractors from Manchester, New Hampshire. The first floor of the new building was furnished with equipment purchased from the Vermont Farm Machinery Company of Bellows Falls, Vermont, and from Moseley & Stoddard of Rutland, Vermont. Apartments for eight Sisters were built upstairs. By 1919, however, Elder Arthur Bruce decided that the dairy herds could no longer be maintained at the village, and they were sold the following year. This scene may therefore be the last view of the Canterbury Shakers packaging butter for sale.

Casseroles[1]

"Arrangements have been made to have the men who work for us have their meals over at the Lodge. A kitchen has been fixed in the two small south rooms. The stove taken from [the] Office kitchen is put here—a general outfit provided."

—Josephine E. Wilson,
diary entry, May 4, 1939

As was the custom everywhere, our wood stoves were used not only for heating houses, but also for cooking. In the Family and Office kitchens, the big range had two ovens large enough to cook a ten- or fifteen-pound roast and bake four pies at a time. This stove, of course, was very convenient for both the meat and the pastry cooks. The range was set in cement to make it safe for use.

In 1939 we took the range out of the Office kitchen and put it in the Lodge, where the hired men boarded. Charles Rollins, one of our hired men, was requested to do the cooking for them, as he was a very fine cook and could easily manage the needs of the few who were still working at Canterbury at that time. In place of the large range, a small wood stove was provided for us, as we were cooking for only three Sisters and occasional visitors.[2] The new stove was much more difficult to use because it had only one oven, when we had been used to two, and it had a smaller surface on which to cook. The one advantage was that it had a little well for water, so there was always hot water available.

However, in 1940, I was surprised one day when coming into the Office to hear Sister Josephine say, "There's a new baby downstairs." I could not imagine what she meant at first. But, on descending to the kitchen, I found she had provided a new electric stove. As the Shakers believed in progress, it was not uncommon for us to obtain new things that required a lot less work.

When we first obtained this stove, there was another innovation coming into the cooking area, called "casseroles." These are very convenient because they can be made ahead and frozen, if necessary. And they do use up leftovers at times, if you have any that can be saved. The following recipe was the first one I made after receiving the new electric stove:

Eldress Bertha's Tuna Casserole

1 large can of tuna
1 large can of shrimp
1 10-ounce can of cream of chicken soup
1 10-ounce can of cream of mushroom soup

3 ounces wide noodles, cooked
½ cup (generous) cheese, grated
Dash cayenne pepper
1 cup crumbs (croutons), buttered

Mix tuna, shrimp, soups, and noodles together in a buttered casserole. Cover with cheese, and sprinkle with cayenne pepper and crumbs. Bake at 400 degrees until golden brown, about ½ hour.

Serves 4–6   *—Shaker Tested Recipes*

Vegetable Pie with Rice Crust

1 cup carrots, sliced	*2 cups potatoes, cubed*
¼ cup onion, chopped	*4 tablespoons butter*
1 green pepper, chopped	*4 tablespoons flour*
1 cup turnips, cubed	*1 teaspoon salt*
1½ cup celery, chopped	*1 cup milk*

Cook all vegetables except potatoes in salted water for 15 minutes. Add potatoes. Cook until tender. Drain. Melt butter, and add flour, salt, milk, and vegetables. Put in casserole and cover with rice crust. Bake at 400 degrees for 20 minutes.

Rice Crust

1 cup rice, boiled	*1 tablespoon sugar*
⅓ cup milk	*1 teaspoon baking powder*
2 eggs, separated	*½ teaspoon salt*
1½ cups flour	*1 tablespoon butter, melted*

Mix rice and milk. Beat yolks and add to rice mixture. Sift dry ingredients and add to mixture with butter. Beat well and fold in beaten egg whites.

Serves 4   *— Shaker Tested Recipes*

The following three recipes come from my *Mennonite Community Cookbook* which was given to me by Barry Roche. He has been a friend of the Shakers for many years, and he and his wife used to come up and help at the gift shop every summer.

Chicken Casserole

2 cups bread cubes, soft
2 cups chicken, cooked, diced
2 tablespoons parsley,
   chopped
1 teaspoon salt

¼ teaspoon pepper
2 eggs, beaten
1½ cups chicken broth
1½ cups milk

Place a layer of bread cubes in a greased casserole dish. Add a layer of chicken, parsley, and seasonings. Mix eggs, milk, and broth and pour over mixture. Bake at 350 degrees for 45 minutes.

Serves 6   —Mrs. J. S. Bucher
                                     Harmon, West Virginia

Cheese and Vegetable Casserole

¼ pound spaghetti
2 cups peas, cooked
1 onion, chopped
1 green pepper, chopped
2 cups tomatoes, canned

1 teaspoon salt
¼ teaspoon pepper
1 cup bread crumbs
1 cup processed cheese, sliced

Cook spaghetti in salt water until tender. Drain. Mix vegetables with seasonings. Place alternate layers of spaghetti and vegetables in a greased casserole dish. Sprinkle with crumbs. Bake at 375 degrees for 35 minutes. Add the sliced cheese and return to oven until cheese is melted.

Serves 6–8   —Mrs. Mary C. Coulson
                                      Hanover, Pennsylvania

Soybean Casserole

2 cups soybeans, dried
2 quarts water, cold
¼ cup bacon, diced
2 cups celery, diced
2 tablespoons onion, minced
2 tablespoons green pepper,
   diced

6 tablespoons flour
2 teaspoons salt
⅛ teaspoon pepper
2 cups milk
1 cup bread crumbs, soft

Soak beans overnight in sufficient water to cover. Drain in the morning and add 2 quarts water. Cook slowly until beans are soft. Fry bacon until light brown and add celery, onion, and green pepper. When vegetables are tender, add flour, salt, and pepper. Gradually add the milk and stir until thickened. Remove from heat and add soybeans. Pour into a casserole and top with bread crumbs. Bake at 350 degrees for 35 minutes.

Serves 6

—Stella Huber Stauffer
Tofield, Alberta, Canada

Plate 10. The Dwelling House kitchen, c. 1937. *Shaker Archives, PN191, SVI.*

The Dwelling House is the second oldest structure in the village, built in 1793, after the Meeting House was completed.

Summer Squash Casserole

2 pounds yellow summer
squash, sliced (about 6
cups)
1 10-ounce can cream of
chicken soup

2 medium onions, sliced
1 cup sour cream
8 ounces (or more) herb-
seasoned bread stuffing or
croutons
½ cup margarine, melted

Cook squash and onion in boiling, salted water for 5 minutes; drain. Combine soup and sour cream, and fold into vegetables. Combine stuffing and margarine. Spread half of stuffing in bottom of 8″ x 8″ x 2″ baking dish. Spoon vegetable mixture on top. Sprinkle remaining stuffing over vegetables. Bake at 350 degrees for 25 to 30 minutes until heated through.

Serves 4   —Nola Stokes, 1980

Plate 11.   Emma King in the Syrup Shop, northwest corner, south room, first floor, c. 1929. *Shaker Archives, 1–PN545, SVI.*

Hamburger Casserole

½ cup onion, diced
2 tablespoons butter
2 potatoes, large
1 pound hamburger
1 bouillon cube
¾ cup water, heated

1 cup celery, diced
1 cup carrots, sliced (about 3
  carrots)
1½ teaspoons salt
⅛ teaspoon pepper

Sauté onion in butter in a large skillet, about 5 minutes. Meanwhile, boil and mash potatoes. Add meatto onion and cook until brown. Soak bouillon cube in hot water. Drain meat. Add bouillon, vegetables, and seasonings to beef mixture. Cover and cook 15 minutes. Mix 1 tablespoon flour and cold water and add to beef mixture. Stir until mixture thickens and put in 9″ x 5″ x 3″ baking dish. Add mashed potatoes on top. Bake at 350 degrees for 30 minutes.

Serves 4-6
—Bertha Lindsay's notes,
Shaker Archives, SVI

Plate 12. Picnic with guests at the Ice Mill Pond, c. 1924. Bertha Lindsay *(far left)*, Miriam Wall *(foreground)*, *Shaker Archives, 1–PN82, SVI.*

In the twentieth century, the Ice Mill Pond area often served as a place for repast. Several mills had occupied the site since 1802. In 1876, the Canterbury Shakers built a structure that housed a threshing mill and an ice house. In 1929 the building was used primarily for storage.

Omelets[1]

"Mr. Whiston is caring for our hens, and they are laying thirty dozen eggs per week, so we have stopped buying, and [are] using home eggs."

—Josephine E. Wilson,
diary entry, December 27, 1939

*S*upper, at the end of the day, was generally a light meal. In the winter, sometimes, we made omelets for supper. These were well liked and can be made very tasty by adding a half a cup of cheese, asparagus, or bits of cooked, diced bacon.

After supper, when we were young, we would have singing groups, prayer services, and other activities. It would be good to explain how some of our evenings, before the days of radio and television, were spent. On Monday evenings, we played games, whatever we wanted to do. In the summer, we would play croquet, shuttlecock, or drop the handkerchief. In the winter, we would play Parcheesi, lotto, or Chinese marbles. Tuesday evenings were given over to the young people's singing group, and we were taught the rudiments of music and how to sing well. On Wednesdays, we had what the Shakers called a "young people's conference." This was given over to the instruction of the rules and regulations or laws that we would all learn together to form a well-disciplined home. Sometimes, if we were not having the instructions presented to us, we would have a prayer service. Thursday evening was when all the Brothers and Sisters came

together and had a nice family singing gathering. At this
time, we usually presented the songs that we had learned in
our different vocal groups. Friday evenings we could spend
as we chose. On Saturday evenings we had another prayer
service. And then, of course, our Sunday worship and
Sunday School came on the following day. In the afternoon,
we sometimes had a young people's prayer service, and, in
the summertime, we held it in the Old Church,[2] which was
such a lovely place to have a service. On Sunday evenings,
Sister Lillian Phelps would start playing the piano, and,
before long, many of the younger people came in to join her
in singing. We often sang gospel songs because we learned
the songs of other churches as well as our own.

Then, when the radios came in, Brother Irving Greenwood
built a crystal set, and made the loudspeaker for it. (See plate
12.) He would have us gather into the chapel to hear the
radio when he was able to come up to play it for us. It had
always been the custom of the Shakers to close the evening at
nine o'clock and retire for the night, so to be able to rise early
that next morning. But the new radio put a stop to all of that,
regardless of the counsels! There were quite long dramas on
the radio, often lasting three to four hours. They were like
regular storybooks and so interesting that once you started
listening you couldn't stop until the end. Those who were
brave enough would sit up on the long benches and listen to
the dramas for that length of time. Sometimes this kept us up
until after one o'clock in the morning. And then, of course,
as the years went on, there were radios bought for the
different rooms, and then still later, for every Sister. It was
quite a thrill when radios came in. It seemed like Jules
Verne's prophecy was coming into reality. And then, of
course, when television came in, we were allowed to have it
in our different houses. Television has brought many
instructive and educational programs, and these are the ones
we particularly like to listen to.

The Shakers believed in a well-rounded education; not
only in book learning, but in every facet of human
experience that would create a perfect whole. Before we can
become spiritual, the basic principles of everyday life must
be learned. Creating our own "heaven on earth" is our aim.

Fluffy Omelet

6 eggs, separated	⅛ teaspoon baking powder
Pinch salt	Salt and pepper, to taste
¼ teaspoon flour	6 tablespoons milk

Beat the egg whites until very stiff, adding a pinch of salt. Beat the egg yolks well and add the flour, baking powder, seasonings, and milk. Carefully fold in the whites and put into a well-buttered omelet pan or fry pan, which is moderately hot. Cook on top of the stove until the egg has begun to set on the bottom of the pan. Slip in the oven at 425 degrees until the whites are set and dry. Fold over and serve immediately.

Serves 3   *—Shaker Tested Recipes*

Plate 13.   Canterbury Shakers at the Syrup Shop with the Baked Bean truck, c. 1930–1940. Eleanor Parmentor *(left)*, Evelyn Polsey *(center)*, Aida Elam *(right)*. *Shaker Archives, P255, SVI.*

The Baked Sweet Omelet, used frequently at our table, also makes a delicious supper dish. The Sabbathday Lake Shakers in Maine often added the blossoms and leaves of the chive plant to the omelet.

Baked Sweet Omelet

4 eggs, separated
¼ teaspoon salt
2⅔ tablespoons flour
1½ cups milk

⅓ teaspoon baking powder
Brown or white sugar
Butter, melted

Beat egg whites until stiff, adding salt. Beat yolks and add flour, milk, and baking powder and blend well. Fold in whites. Bake in a greased pan in thin rounds of 2–3 tablespoons each. Bake at 375–400 degrees for 3–5 minutes. To serve, sprinkle each round with sugar and butter, and layer 2–3 rounds for each serving. Makes a lovely, light meal or accompaniment to vegetables.

Serves 2

—Shaker Tested Recipes

Plate 14. "Bill of Fare," a song written for a program performed by Jessie Evans, Jennie Fish, and Cora Helena Sarle, c. 1912–1937. *Shaker Archives, Ms. 939, SVI.*

Baked Apple Omelet

4 eggs
½ teaspoon salt
2 tablespoons sugar
½ cup flour
½ cup sour cream
⅓ cup milk

½ cup apple, grated
½ teaspoon lemon peel, grated
1 tablespoon lemon juice
1 tablespoon butter

Beat eggs with salt. Blend in sugar and flour. Beat until smooth and blend in sour cream and milk. Stir in apple, lemon peel, and juice. Pour into hot, buttered frying pan. Bake at 450 degrees in oven until fluffy and brown, about 5 minutes. This is almost like a soufflé. Serve immediately.

Serves 2

—Bertha Lindsay's notes,
Shaker Archives, SVI

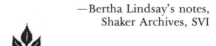

Plate 15. Industrial parade, garden entry, west of the Dwelling House, July 6, 1916. (Probably) Muriel Hewitt, center. *Shaker Archives, 1–PN161, SVI.*

The Canterbury Shakers offered many "entertainments" in the early twentieth century. On July 6, 1916, the Shakers held their own Independence Day parade. (The occasion had been postponed for two days, due to rain.) From two until three o'clock, the costumed participants promenaded throughout the Church Family site, each representing one of the trades or some other important aspect of the community. At four-thirty in the afternoon, the Shakers ended the festivities with a "Mother Goose's Grab Bag Party."

Pictured here is the "garden float." Real pots and pans and facsimiles made of fabric and paper as well as smiling paper potatoes and apples decorate the wagons. One young resident *(center)* is dressed as a chef; another *(right)* is wearing an outfit that resembles a canning jar filled with peas. This entry won second prize.

Vegetables[1]

"*Within the last week, twenty-two acres of potatoes have been planted. The work has been done with a tractor and potato planter. We sold an old tractor to get this machine. The potatoes are all engaged by the Merrimac Farmers Exchange.*"

—Josephine E. Wilson,
diary entry, June 6, 1939

Quite a few acres of land were bought in Concord by the Canterbury Shakers in the early years. One plot of land, called Intervale, is now partly occupied by a motel and a shopping mall,[2] but was where, until the 1930s, we raised acres of squash, potatoes, and occasionally corn. This produce was raised for home consumption and for sale. We have always believed in having plenty of vegetables and fruit. We were very self-sufficient in growing all of these things so as to provide for the Family in both the summer and in the winter.

Sister Rebecca Hathaway had the responsibility of picking the fruits and vegetables, such as peas, beans, spinach, onions, and beets, at our garden at the village. When things were ready to pick, she would ask the Sisters to come and help. Muriel Hewitt and I were appointed to help her at the Canning House.[3] Before she had the responsibility of preserving the fruits and vegetables, this process took place in the Laundry under Sister Amanda Mathews' supervision. All of the Sisters came out to prepare the vegetables and fruits for canning, but I helped Sister Rebecca do this work for thirty years. In fact, she taught me how to make jellies and jams, and we made various lots of pickles and relishes for sale, too. Sometimes we would process three thousand cans of fruits and vegetables, and these were stored away for the winter. I enjoyed doing this work because I love to cook, and this was really a happy experience for me. (See plate 16.)

In the beginning, I understand, that berries—one of the first of the canning fruits—were put into jugs for preservation. Later, of course, glass canning jars came out with a top of metal and a porcelain interior. Then the cold pack method of processing fruits and vegetables appeared, and the

Plate 16.   Bertha Lindsay in the Syrup Shop, east wall, first floor, c. 1935. *Shaker Archives, 1-PN488, SVI.*

Bertha began to be involved with the canning when she was a teenager, about 1912. At that time, the Shakers made jams and jellies for their own use as well as for sale. At one point, Sister Rebecca Hathaway, who was in charge of that duty, fell ill, and recommended that Bertha take over the job. Soon afterwards, the Shakers received a request from a customer for a case of currant jelly. Thus began one of the first canning projects she managed alone.

Shakers, believing in progress, took up this method. I have found, however, that the hot pack method was perhaps the most efficient and less time-consuming than the other methods, and so this was used in canning our fruits for many years. Later, of course, freezers came in, and we think that the freezer is really one of the best ways to preserve food if it is not kept too long.

In the 1930s and 1940s, some of the Sisters had a wonderful idea. If they could sell baked beans and brown bread, they would help very much in augmenting our income. Sisters Aida Elam and Evelyn Polsey, with the help of Gertrude Roberts and Eleanor Parmenter, were the ones who baked the beans and brown bread. Sister Rebecca was elected to make the pickles, as she was the canner. Muriel and I assisted Rebecca in making a variety of pickles to go with the baked beans. (See plate 17.)

The baked beans were cooked in an oven with revolving shelves, the picture of which was placed on cartons to show people where the pots of beans were baked.[4] (See plate 17.) A truck, decorated with an image of the oven, was provided to take the produce around for sale. Eunice Clark and another Sister, probably Aida, sold the beans, and Charles Kinney drove the car around wherever they wanted to go. (See plate 15.) At first, they travelled throughout the neighborhood and into Concord where the goods were peddled right from the truck. Later, as the weather grew a little colder, the Sisters were permitted to go into one or two of the stores and have a counter on which to place these articles for sale. In Concord, the Sisters had a table at Fitch's Drug Store[5] where they could sell the beans. In 1952 the advertising sign for the truck was sold.

Vegetables were plentiful at the village, so it was an easy task to plan menus, which were wholesome and good, although simple. The way the Shakers prepared vegetables started before my day and has been passed down from several cooks. The following dishes are some of the favorite recipes I have used throughout my cooking days.

Plate 17. Evelyn Polsey at the bake oven with revolving shelves, Dwelling House bakery, c. 1940. *Shaker Archives, SVI.*

The crocks of baked beans *(pictured, left)* cooked overnight in the oven. In this scene, Evelyn Polsey is filling cardboard cannisters with the beans, which were to be sold in Concord.

Parsnips are a specialty of the Shakers.

Canterbury Shaker Parsnips

8 parsnips (size of carrots)
¼ cup brown sugar
1 stick butter

Peel and cut parsnips in half. Cook in salted water until tender. Drain. Butter cookie sheet well. Lay parsnips on it, cover with brown sugar, and dot with butter. Brown just a trifle in the oven to make them look pretty.

Serves 6–8

Sweet Potatoes

3 sweet potatoes, medium
Butter
1 can apricots, medium (or 3
fresh pears, ½ cup
cranberry sauce, sprinkle of
brown sugar)

Peel and boil sweet potatoes until tender. Slice potatoes in rounds and put in buttered baking dish (about 9" x 5" x 3" size). Add apricots and pour apricot juice from can on top. Dot with a little butter. Bake in oven about 20 minutes at 350 degrees to heat thoroughly. This recipe can be varied. Instead of apricots, peel, core, and cut up raw pears in large chunks. Drop teaspoonfuls of cranberry sauce on top. Sprinkle with a little brown sugar.

Serves 6   —Margaretta Thompson, 1958

Pleasant Hill Baked Eggplant

1 eggplant, large
1 onion, small, chopped
2 tablespoons butter
3 tablespoons parsley,
    chopped

Dash Worcestershire sauce
Salt and pepper, to taste
2 cups cracker crumbs,
    coarsely ground
1 can cream of mushroom soup

Cut eggplant in half lengthwise. Scrape out the inside, leaving about ½" around sides and bottom of each shell. Boil eggplant meat in salted water until tender. Drain. Sauté onion in butter and add parsley. Mix parsley and onion mixture with eggplant and soup. Add seasonings. Mix with enough crackers to make a good stuffing consistency. Pile filling back into the eggplant shells. Sprinkle with remaining crumbs and dot with butter. Bake at 375 degrees for 30 to 35 minutes.

Serves 4   —adapted from Elizabeth C. Kremer,
                                         We Make You Kindly Welcome

Baked Tomatoes

3 cups fresh tomatoes (or 28
    ounces canned, crushed
    tomatoes)
1 teaspoon salt
⅛ teaspoon black pepper
3 tablespoons sugar

2 tablespoons butter
½ cup (scant) grated mild
    cheddar cheese
1 cup bread crumbs (or
    croutons), buttered

Place tomatoes in a greased baking dish. Add salt, pepper, and sugar. Melt butter and rub into crumbs. Sprinkle crumbs on top of tomatoes. Bake at 350 degrees for 35 minutes. Add grated cheese during last 10 minutes of cooking.

Serves 6   —Mrs. Harry Lambertson, in Mary Emma
                                   Showalter, *Mennonite Community Cookbook*

The Shakers served their turnips this way.

Canterbury Shaker Turnips

3 turnips, small (serves 2–
  4), or 2 turnips, large
  (serves 7)
1–2 tablespoons sugar
  (to taste)

½ teaspoon salt
¼ pound butter
¼ cup cream (to taste)

This recipe will require using a flour bag or cheese cloth, a grinder or food mill, and a double boiler. Peel and cut turnips into finger lengths. Cook until tender. Drain and put in a grinder or food mill. Put mixture in a flour bag or cheese cloth; drain overnight. Squeeze out all water. Add sugar, salt, and butter, and enough cream to swell it out. The turnips should still be good and dry. Put in a double boiler to warm.

Serves 2–7

Artichokes and Mushrooms

1 cup fresh mushrooms
Butter
1 13-ounce can artichokes,
  drained
1 cup white sauce (see page 61)

1 cup (generous) shredded
  cheese
Dash cayenne pepper
Dash paprika

Quarter mushrooms, if large. Sauté mushrooms in a little butter. Add artichokes, white sauce, and cheese. Put in a buttered baking dish. Sprinkle a little bit of cayenne pepper and paprika on top. Bake at 375 degrees until bubbly, about 20 minutes.

Serves 4   —John Auchmoody, 1979

Sister Aida may have used pork in her baked beans; I don't know. I serve pork at the table, but I don't add it to my baked beans.

Eldress Bertha's Baked Beans

2 cups pea beans (or any
   kind of bean)
2 teaspoons salt
¼ teaspoon pepper
1 teaspoon baking soda
1 teaspoon (scant) summer
   savory, dried (optional)

2 tablespoons molasses
   (not black strap)
¼ cup maple syrup
1 whole onion, small
1 stick of margarine

Put the beans in a pot to soak overnight in cold water. The next morning, heat to parboiling. Then take them off and drain the beans. In a pot, put salt, pepper, soda, summer savory, molasses, maple syrup, and the whole onion. Add the beans. Pour fresh boiling water over them, a little more than just to cover them. Put the beans into the oven and bake at 225 degrees for six hours. When you take them out, remove the onion and add the stick of margarine. I recently tried adding the summer savory because it makes the beans easier to digest.

Serves 8

—Quoted to the editor, 1986

Plate 18. Onions from the Canterbury Shaker vegetable garden, c. 1942–1947. *Shaker Archives, PN246, SVI.*

Beginning in 1942, Bertha Lindsay, Miriam Wall, and Mildred Wells began to work on a Victory Garden. Their effort "to help [the] brave boys in the service [and] to restore this world to sanity again," lasted five years. The garden plot was composed of three acres, with forty-five rows of plants, each row being three hundred feet long. The Sisters planted broccoli, four kinds of beans, beets, cabbages, carrots, cauliflower, celery, sweet corn, cucumbers, eggplant, garlic, lettuce, watermelons, musk melons, onions, parsley, parsnips, peppers, peas, radishes, spinach, squash, tomatoes, potatoes, and turnips. The garden supplied the thirty Canterbury Sisters, hired hands, and friends with produce. In addition, the Sisters were able to sell some of the vegetables to subsidize the project. In 1943 they sold one hundred bushels of table onions and sixteen bushels of pickling onions, and they made enough of a profit to enable them to purchase all of the plants they needed for the following year, as well as new blackberry, blueberry, and raspberry bushes and strawberry plants.

Salads[1]

"Girls transplanting 6,930 onions, including onion sets and seeds. 18,700 onions are now on the way."

—Ida Crook, *diary entry, May 30, 1944*

I do not know the exact date that salads became popular, but here at Canterbury, while we had all the ingredients for a salad, like lettuce, cucumbers, celery, radishes, tomatoes, and onions, they were all served separately. The members would have the makings of it and would make it themselves at the table, but we cooks wouldn't make a salad as often for the Family as we would for company. We often served bowls of lettuce with vinegar and sugar. It wasn't until the 1930s that, like everyone else, we combined different vegetables as a salad, and then it became quite the thing to make gelatin salads, which are always appropriate to add to a menu. Cucumbers and lettuce were particularly plentiful and were served right through the season of their growing for both dinner and supper, so that everyone had all he or she wanted of these two vegetables.

Cucumbers, of course, were also used for pickling. Sometimes there would be gallons of sour pickles for use at the village, as well as sweet pickles, and sweet relishes for the public to buy. We sold many kinds of pickles at our Bazaar at the Schoolhouse, but I don't know whether I can remember them all. We used to put horseradish and grape leaves on the top and bottom of the crock to give a little flavor to the vinegar. We had plenty of horseradish growing around the village, and we made horseradish for sale. We also made beet relish, and this was combined with horseradish, which made a very nice flavor.

I think the pickling season was the most interesting time of the year. There was such a nice smell in the kitchens where

Plate 19. Sister Rebecca Hathaway *(right)* and two assistants, Bertha Lindsay *(far left)* and *(probably)* Muriel Hewitt *(center),* in the Syrup Shop, southwest corner, north room, first floor, c. 1913–1935. *Shaker Archives, 11–P269, SVI.*

In this photograph, the room is carefully arranged in an attempt to document the mileau of the Kitchen Deaconess. One can sense the pride Rebecca felt in her domain; the glistening apples are lined up in one corner ready to be peeled and chopped, and each item is stored in an orderly way. Even the apprentices in the background are perched awkwardly in their chairs, as if poised for action. In the adjoining room streamers of flypaper drape the ceiling, and an unrelated machine (used to cut fancywork that was made for sale) has been hidden with a cloth. Although the room underwent many changes prior to 1922 to make improvements for the canning activities, no major changes occurred after that time.

the pickles were being made, and many times, when company was walking around, they would come in and sniff and enjoy the nice smells. We always had such a good time making pickles, and I'm sure that many of our visitors had a good time eating them as well.

Bewitching Salad

2 3-ounce packages lemon
  gelatin
2 cups boiling water
1 bottle ginger ale (16
  ounces)
Juice of 1 lemon
1 cup celery, finely diced
1 cup grapes, chopped
1 cup blanched nut meats, chopped

2 cups white chicken meat,
  diced
1 cup sweet pepper, finely
  shredded
Salad oil
Lettuce
Mayonnaise, to taste

Add gelatin to boiling water; cool and stir in ginger ale. Add lemon juice. When partially congealed, add celery, grapes, nuts, chicken, and pepper, and pour into mold rubbed with salad oil. Chill until firm. Serve on crisp lettuce with mayonnaise.

Serves 8

—*Shaker Tested Recipes*

Plate 20.   (See following page.) Vegetable garden, looking west at the Laundry, garden tractor in the foreground. *Shaker Archives, 1– PN548, SVI.*

Canary Salad

1 cup carrot, grated
½ cup apple, chopped
½ cup celery, cut into small
   pieces

½ cup orange, peeled and
   sectioned
2 tablespoons mayonnaise
Lettuce

Mix vegetables and fruit together and combine with mayonnaise. Serve on lettuce.

Serves 4   *—Shaker Tested Recipes*

Carrot and Pineapple Salad

1 3-ounce package lemon
   gelatin
1 cup boiling water
1 cup pineapple juice
1 cup crushed pineapple,
   drained well

1½ cups carrots, grated
½ cup nuts, chopped
Salad oil
Lettuce
Mayonnaise

Dissolve gelatin in hot water and add pineapple juice. Chill. When this begins to thicken, add other ingredients. Pour mixture into a mold rubbed with salad oil. Chill until set. Unmold on lettuce. Serve with mayonnaise. (It is possible to use the juice from the drained pineapple for 1 cup pineapple juice, if desired.)

Serves 6   —Mary Emma Showalter,
                                   Mennonite Community Cookbook

Frosted Honeydew Salad

1 honeydew melon, medium size
1 package raspberry gelatin,
   3 ounces
1 can fruit cocktail, 16
   ounces (or 2 cups fresh
   fruit, cut up)

1 8-ounce package cream
   cheese
Milk
Lettuce
Salad dressing (optional)

Peel melon and cut slice from one end. Remove seeds. Fill cavity with water, then use that water, brought to a boil, for dissolving a package of raspberry gelatin. When gelatin is somewhat thickened, fold in well-drained canned fruit cocktail or cut-up fruit. Fill the melon and place in refrigerator until gelatin is firm. Soften cream cheese with a little milk and whip it fluffy. Frost the melon with the cheese and place on serving plate with crisp lettuce. Serve slices; top with a salad dressing. Omit the dressing, and you have a delicious dessert.

Serves 10

—Shaker Tested Recipes

Macaroni Vegetable Salad

2 cups macaroni, cooked
½ cup peas, cooked
½ cup string beans, cooked
½ cup carrot, raw, grated

2 tablespoons onion, raw,
   grated
French dressing
Lettuce

Mix the macaroni and vegetables and marinate with French dressing. Serve on lettuce.

Serves 6

—Shaker Tested Recipes

Golden Salad

2 tablespoons gelatin	1 cup carrot, grated
1 cup cold water	1 cup celery, cut fine
2 cups boiling water	1 cup pineapple, crushed or
¾ cup sugar	diced and drained
1 teaspoon salt	Lettuce
½ cup lemon juice	Mayonnaise

Soak gelatin in cold water, then dissolve in boiling water. Add sugar and salt and stir until dissolved. Add lemon juice. Allow gelatin to cool, then place in refrigerator until thickened slightly. Add carrot, celery, and pineapple, and turn into wet molds. Chill and serve on lettuce with mayonnaise or cream dressing.

Serves 6   *—Shaker Tested Recipes*

Sauces and Dressings[1]

"Cutting apples for drying was commenced in the Laundry by Brethren and Sisters two evenings in a week and sometimes three; 20–40 bushels an evening. Finished Oct. 31. The Church harvested 4,000 bushels of apples. A large store was laid in for Fall and Winter use; a portion of them was ground into cider to convert into vinegar, boil down for applesauce, &c."

—Anonymous, *"Church Record II,"*
Canterbury, August 2, 1876

*M*any varieties of fruit trees were planted here. We had, at one time, a pear orchard, located on the Ice Mill Pond Road. In Dorothy Durgin's day, we had what we called "the peach orchard" on the other side of the cow lane from the Barn. Later, peach trees were planted between the apple trees at the North Family. In 1942, Mildred Wells and I planted peach stones in front of Enfield House. There were cherry trees, plum trees, and pear trees around the village in many places, adding a beautiful picture in the spring, but also giving us delicious fruit to eat raw, to can, and to make into sauces.

The sale of apples was part of the Canterbury Shakers' livelihood in the early days. Apple-picking season was a very exciting time, and the Sisters and most of the young people participated in the work. It was fun to see who had the courage to climb to the top of the ladder to pick the apples, because some of us would not. It was very handy for us to have a basket with a hook attached so that we could hang it on the ladder and use both hands for picking. (See plate 21.) And there was always a Brother around to take the basket of apples to empty into a bushel basket when we were through. The apples had to be handled very gently so as not to mar them, because these were sold to markets, some as far off as England.

The apples were brought from the orchards to Sisters waiting outside the cellar of the Sisters' Shop door. (See plate 24.) We would sit down in the very low, little chairs provided especially for this purpose and could easily pick over the apples. The apples were graded from what we called "Number One" to "Number Three." The Number One apples were sold, the Number Two apples were stored for the table, and the Number Three apples were used first because they were not good keepers.

There were three different apple cellars provided with bins about two feet high, made of long strips of wood. These bins were screened to prevent mice from getting in. The bins had plenty of air and were kept at just such a temperature in order to preserve the apples for as long as possible.

Many of the apples in the early days were dried for winter use or were made into the famous Shaker applesauce. The apples were cored and pared by the Brothers on a little apple corer, then passed on to the Sisters who made sure that the cores were entirely out and that there were no skins left on. The Sisters at the Dry House[2] then took charge of the apples, staying up all night to keep the fire at an even temperature to dry the apples slowly. The apples were dried through very well and then were stored in wooden chests to keep them until ready for use. The applesauce was sold in little firkins for many years. The firkins were made in two different sizes, and each had on the top of the cover a picture of the apple and stated where the apples were raised and cooked. So this was always a very fun time for the young people, because there was always something doing.

Sometimes we had applesauce morning and night. I grew up making applesauce. Nothing was written down. We had plenty of apples to use, so we used them in any and every possible form.[3] At the end of the season, the apples were not so tasty.

Plate 21. Canterbury Shakers sorting apples at the Sisters' Shop, east entrance, c. 1929. Emma King *(second from left)*. *Shaker Archives, P126, SVI.* During fair weather, the Sisters cored and peeled fresh produce there. In the background is the North Shop, where the Sisters stored their cloaks for sale and operated the fancywork industry.

Shaker, or Boiled Cider, Applesauce

1 bushel sweet apples
1 gallon boiled cider

Put the cider into a brass or tin boiler. Wash and drain the apples; put them into the boiler, and cover tight. If the boiler will hold one bushel of apples, two hours should be given for cooking. Care should be taken that they do not cling to the boiler or scorch. Cook very slowly over a moderate but steady heat. Do not stir the apples while cooking.

—Mary Whitcher, *Shaker House-Keeper*

Although I prefer to use Baldwin apples for this dish, I remember we sometimes used the Golden Ball. The Golden Ball apple was so large, a single dish of applesauce could be made from it.

Eldress Bertha's Applesauce

4 apples, large, Baldwin
¼ cup sugar
½ cup water

3 tablespoons cinnamon drops ("redhots"), or 1 teaspoon almond extract

Peel, core, and chop apples coarsely. Mix first three ingredients together. Cook until apples are softened. Time will vary on type of apples used. Add more water if the apples are Northern Spies; add a little less if the apples are MacIntosh or Cortlands. Add cinnamon "hots" or almond extract after cooking, but while still hot. Stir until dissolved or well mixed.

Makes 2 cups   —Quoted to the editor, 1985

Sister Eunice Clarke's Lemon Sauce

1 cup granulated sugar
2 tablespoons plus 2
   teaspoons cornstarch
2 tablespoons lemon rind, grated

2 cups boiling water
6 tablespoons lemon juice
2 teaspoons butter or
   margarine

Blend together the sugar, cornstarch, and lemon rind in the top of a double boiler. Add boiling water and cook 15 minutes over hot water. Add lemon juice and butter. Serve hot.

Makes 2 cups   —Notes, Shaker Archives, SVI

Custard Sauce

3 egg yolks, lightly beaten   *2 cups milk, heated, but not*
2 tablespoons sugar   *boiling*

Combine yolks and sugar. Stir a little milk into the
yolks; slowly return yolks into the milk, stirring or
whisking constantly. Do not allow the custard to boil or
get too hot, as the eggs will curdle. Keep it at medium or
low heat until the mixture coats the spoon. Use a
double boiler if possible. Pour into a bowl to cool. Serve
over and around the Grape Sponge Pudding (page 82)
(if the pudding is made in a mold).

Makes 2 cups   —Notes, Shaker Archives, SVI

Plate 22.   Canterbury Sisters on their way to pick apples, west of
the Trustees' Office and Wood Shed, October, 1918. Sister
Florence Phelps *(foreground)*, Bertha Lindsay *(far right, next to cab)*,
Ethel Hudson *(on Bertha's right)*, Edith Green *(third from left)*. *Shaker
Archives, 1–PN110, SVI.*

   The baskets depicted here were either commercially manufactured or were made at other Shaker communities. The
Canterbury Shakers made only about one hundred baskets, and
they stopped their production in 1848. The one held by Florence
Phelps pictured here had a hook attached so that the person who
was picking fruit could hang the basket on a tree branch and could
work with both arms free.

Hard Sauce

1 stick margarine, at room
   temperature
1 cup confectioners sugar
1 teaspoon vanilla

Cream the margarine. Add sugar gradually, beating until fluffy. Chill. This recipe can be made beforehand. Remove from the refrigerator about one hour before serving to soften. Serve with the Troy Pudding or the Steamed Chocolate Pudding. (See pages 79 and 84.)

Makes 1 cup   —Quoted to the editor, 1986

Tarragon Dressing

⅔ cup sugar (a little less)
1½ cups salad oil
1 cup lemon juice, (or ¼ cup
   lemon juice and ½ cup
   tarragon vinegar, mixed)
1 teaspoon Worcestershire
   sauce
1 teaspoon dry mustard

1 teaspoon salt
2 tablespoons catsup
   (homemade if possible)
2 whole cloves
A little grated onion (or 1
   teaspoon chives, chopped)
1 tablespoon tarragon leaves,
   chopped

Mix all ingredients in order given. Beat well for 2 minutes. Put in bottle and refrigerate. Should stand overnight. Shake well before using. May be strained before using.

Makes about 2½ cups   —Amy Bess Miller and Persis Wellington
                         Fuller, *The Best of Shaker Cooking*

Tomato Sauce

6 tomatoes, medium,
    quartered
4 cloves
1 tablespoon onion, minced
2 tablespoons butter

2 tablespoons flour
Salt and pepper
Dash cayenne pepper
Parsley, minced

Put the tomatoes, cloves, and onion in a stewpot. Cover and cook together 20–30 minutes. Strain through a sieve. Press against tomatoes to extract as much juice as possible. Discard tomatoes. Heat butter in a pan and stir flour into it. Cook, stirring all the time, until smooth and light brown. Stir juice slowly into the pan. Cook 2 or 3 minutes longer. Add seasonings. Sprinkle in parsley at the last minute.

Makes 2 cups

—Adapted from Mary Whitcher's
Shaker House-Keeper

White Sauce

1 tablespoon butter
1 tablespoon flour
1 cup light cream

Dash white pepper
Dash salt

Melt butter in saucepan. Add flour and stir constantly so that the flour won't burn. Cook for 1 to 2 minutes, stirring all the while, then add light cream in a slow, thin stream. Continue cooking and stirring until sauce is hot and begins to come to a boil and thickens. Season to taste.

Makes 1 cup

—Quoted to the editor, 1985

Plate 23. Christmas tree at Canterbury Shaker Village, n.d., *Shaker Archives, PN100, SVI.*

Breads[1]

"We decide to try buying our bread for the summer, as our Sisters are taxed with the care of the sick, and we have not the help we need for the kitchen work. . . . The last bread for our Family was made yesterday by Alice Howland. Twelve loaves of bread come today from Cote Brothers of Manchester. This will reach our mail carrier at noon, and distribution will be made from the office. $5.34 for bread."

—Josephine E. Wilson,
diary entries, April 4–7, 1937

*I*n the early 1800s, the Shakers built a gristmill, and they ground flour, not only for their own use, but also for sale. By the time I came to Canterbury in 1905, the Shakers were buying their flour in bulk. It has seemed to me that the flour of today isn't anything like the flour of bygone days. Today, the flour is bleached, with some properties taken out and others put in. It doesn't seem to provide as fine a textured product. Is that my imagination or not? I do agree that the packaged cakes and muffins are valuable to those who do not know how to cook and to young people just marrying or having to work, who don't have the time to cook from scratch, so I do approve of having the packaged dishes if the right materials are used.

Muffins and biscuits were made for breakfast and for supper, and were well liked by our Family. The young folks were instructed to use everything possible and not to waste anything, as frugality was one of our injunctions. Our founder, Mother Ann, said we should remember the poor and needy and give bread to the hungry. Sometimes we saved our cereal left over from breakfast and made it into muffins for the supper table or for the following breakfast. Squash biscuits were often made, using up the little bit of leftover squash. So many of these things, while they may have been leftovers, were delicious when used in muffins and biscuits.

Many different dessert breads were made through the years. I've always been fond of baking breads of any kind, but in later years, I branched out to German sweet breads. The German breads are delicious; these were mainly what would be called either "coffee cakes" or "tea cakes." I found them very interesting to make, especially the Stollen, which I gave as Christmas presents for many years.

Doughnuts were quite a favorite, too. There were many different kinds, like orange doughnuts and squash dough-nuts, providing a different taste than is generally known. The White Doughnut was popular especially through the Spring, as it was eaten with maple syrup. We made these doughnuts without an egg, however, hence their name. We cut them finger length and handled them as little as possible to keep the dough limber. When fried, the dough formed holes, providing ample space for nice maple syrup to be poured in, to be eaten and enjoyed by all. The raised doughnut and the one rolled in powdered sugar were also favorites.

The following notes are from my scrapbook, which Leona Merrill Rowell used while she was here. After she left, the book was given to me because I was the bread maker. She took the notes from books we had at the bakery.

"Bread Wisdom"

In baking bread, the most important point to consider is the yeast. Keep your yeast with care. Whenever possible, keep it in an icebox, where it will be dry and cold. Though yeast may discolor at times, this in no way impairs its quality. So long as it is firm it is good to use. When it becomes too soft to handle, do not use it.

The Mixing

Measure the liquid into a bowl and add the sugar. Sugar assists fermentation. Next, crumble yeast into the mixture. Allow to stand from six to eight minutes; add the shortening and sift enough flour to form a smooth light batter. Beat this thoroughly, so that the yeast may be well distributed. Salt may be dissolved or used dry.

The Kneading

The dough must not be chilled; therefore, knead quickly and lightly until it is smooth and elastic and does not stick to fingers or board.

The Rising

After kneading, place dough in a bowl and set in a warm place, free from draught. Cover bowl to prevent crust from forming on dough, which would cause a streak in the bread. Let dough rise double in bulk.

The Molding

Next, mold bread into loaves about half the size of pans. Put each loaf in a well-greased pan and let rise again in a warm place, free from draughts until double in size. To test if loaf is ready for oven, flour the finger and make an impression in loaf. If the impression disappears, give a little more time; if it remains, bread is ready to bake.

The Baking

Place in a quick oven where the loaf should brown in from fifteen to twenty minutes, then reduce the heat and bake more slowly. Bread is done when it leaves the sides of the pan. An ordinary-sized loaf will bake in from forty to fifty minutes. A large loaf should bake in one hour. Biscuits, rolls, etc., require a hotter oven than bread and should be baked in fifteen or twenty minutes.

Helpful Hints

Sponges should not be permitted to get too light. They are ready when bubbles gather on surface and break occasionally.

After the loaf is baked, remove from pan and let it stand out of a draught until cold.

To freshen stale bread, dip it in cold water, then rebake in a quick oven.

Shaker Raised Squash Biscuits

1 cup milk
4 tablespoons butter or
*   margarine*
¾ cup sugar
½ teaspoon salt
1 yeast cake
*   (or 1 envelope of dry yeast)*

4–5 cups flour
1½ cups butternut squash,
*   strained (or 1 16-ounce*
*   can of squash)*
2 eggs, room temper(

In small saucepan, heat milk and butter to very hot. Mix sugar and salt in large bowl and pour in milk. Let sugar/milk mixture cool until lukewarm. Add yeast and 2 cups flour. Beat at medium speed in a mixer for 2 minutes. Add squash and eggs. Mix well. Continue to add flour (with wooden spoon) until you have a stiff dough; the dough should begin to leave the sides of the bowl. Turn out onto a floured board and knead 7–8 minutes, using additional flour on the board to prevent sticking. Put back in cleaned, greased bowl. Turn dough greased side up and cover with a towel. Let rise in a warm place until double. Punch dough down and turn out. Shape into biscuits. Place in square 8″ x 8″ pan for soft sides; in muffin pans; or shape into cloverleaf rolls. Let rise double again. Bake in preheated 400-degree oven until brown, about 25 minutes. Butter tops while hot.

Makes 2½–3 dozen   —Bertha Lindsay's scrapbook, c. 1938

Eldress Bertha's Rice Muffins

2½ cups flour
2 tablespoons sugar
1 teaspoon salt (if rice is
    leftover and was cooked in
    salted water, use ½
    teaspoon salt)

5 teaspoons baking powder
1 egg
1½ cups milk
2 tablespoons shortening (or
    oil or margarine)
¾ cup rice, cooked

Mix dry ingredients. In a small bowl, beat egg and add 1 cup milk and shortening. Make a well in center of dry ingredients; add liquids; and mix just to moisten. Add rice mixed with ½ cup milk. Mix quickly. Put into greased 2″ muffin tins, filling to ⅔ full. Bake at 400 degrees, 12–15 minutes, until light brown. Remove from tins and cool on rack.

Makes 15–18 muffins   —Bertha Lindsay's scrapbook, c. 1938

Johnny Cakes

¼ cup shortening or margarine
¼ cup sugar
1 cup flour
½ cup cornmeal, stone-ground

4 teaspoons baking powder
½ teaspoon soda
1 egg, beaten
1 cup sour cream

Preheat oven to 375 degrees. Cream together sugar and shortening. Sift dry ingredients together. Mix together egg and sour cream. Add alternately with dry ingredients to creamed mixture. Mix only until moistened. Turn into a greased 8″ square pan. Bake 25 minutes in preheated oven. Cool on rack in pan.

Makes 12 squares   —Bertha Lindsay's "Geography"

Plate 24. Dwelling House dining room, east wall, c. 1914. *Shaker Archives, 14–P3, SVI.*

In 1914, Josephine Wilson ordered "glass topped" tables and wooden chairs for the dining room. The set, pictured here, cost $383.00 and was purchased from Hoitts, a furniture store in Manchester, New Hampshire, about thirty miles south of the village. The Shakers did not approve of the furniture, however,

because the surface of the tables remained cold in the winter months. In 1940 they bought six maple tables and twenty-four chairs from Chase & Co., also of Manchester. The new set cost $173.50 and included an exchange of the unwanted pieces.

The room pictured here is probably arranged as it would have been at a routine meal. The decorative chains that drape from the ceiling are made of flypaper.

Poppy Seed Rolls

¾ cup milk
½ cup butter or margarine
1 envelope dry yeast
¾ cup sugar
1 teaspoon salt
3 eggs, beaten (save 1
    tablespoon to brush tops of
    rolls)

1 teaspoon nutmeg
1 tablespoon flavoring
    (vanilla, orange, or almond)
½ teaspoon orange rind
4½–5 cups flour
1 tablespoon sugar
1 tablespoon milk

Prepare filling (see below). Cool. In saucepan, scald milk and butter. Put sugar and salt in large bowl. Pour in hot milk and stir. Cool to lukewarm. Add yeast and 2 cups of flour and mix, medium speed, 2 minutes. Stir in eggs, nutmeg, flavoring, and orange rind. Stir in remaining flour to make a stiff dough. Divide dough in half. Roll each half out on a slightly floured board as for a jellyroll (about 12″ x 9″). Spread with filling. Roll, starting at wide end. Make slices 1½″ wide, about 10 slices per roll (2 rolls). Place cut side up in 2 greased 9″ x 9″ pans. Brush top with reserved egg, which is mixed with sugar and milk. Cover and place in a warm area. Let rise double. Bake in preheated oven, 325 degrees, 40–45 minutes.

Filling

¾ cup poppy seeds
½ cup raisins
½ cup sugar

⅛ cup milk
1 teaspoon vanilla

Cover poppy seeds with water in small saucepan and soak 1 hour. Bring to a boil, lower heat, and cook, stirring occasionally as water evaporates. Drain thoroughly. Add remaining ingredients.

Makes 2 12″ rolls

—Bertha Lindsay's notes,
Shaker Archives, SVI

Zucchini Walnut Bread

4 eggs, beaten
1½ cups brown sugar,
   packed
¾ cup vegetable oil
3 cups flour
1½ teaspoons baking soda
¾ teaspoon baking powder

¾ teaspoon salt
2 teaspoons cinnamon
2 cups zucchini, unpeeled,
   grated
1 cup walnuts, coarsely
   chopped
1 teaspoon vanilla

Preheat oven to 350 degrees. In a large bowl, mix eggs, sugar, and oil. Sift flour, soda, baking powder, salt, and cinnamon. Stir sifted ingredients into egg mixture. Add zucchini, walnuts, and vanilla. Turn into greased 10″ tube pan or two 9″ bread pans. Bake 50–55 minutes.

—Bertha Lindsay's notes,
Shaker Archives, SVI

Pumpkin Bread

3 cups sugar
1 cup corn oil
4 eggs, beaten
1 can pumpkin (15–16
   ounces)
3½ cups flour
1 teaspoon baking powder

2 teaspoons baking soda
2 teaspoons salt
½ teaspoon cloves
1 teaspoon allspice
1 teaspoon nutmeg
1 teaspoon cinnamon
⅔ cup water

Preheat oven to 350 degrees. Combine sugar and oil. Stir in eggs and pumpkin. Sift together flour, baking powder, and soda with salt and spices. Add to egg mixture alternately with water. Bake at 350 degrees in 2 greased 9″ x 5″ x 3″ pans or in three 8½″ x 4½″ x 2⅝″ pans, for 1 hour and 10 minutes. Cool on rack 15 minutes. Turn out. Cool completely.

—Bertha Lindsay's scrapbook

Stollen

1 cup seedless raisins
1 cup (8-ounce jar) mixed,
  chopped candied fruits
¼ cup orange juice
¾ cup milk
½ cup sugar
1 teaspoon salt
1 cup (2 sticks) butter or
  margarine
2 envelopes active dry yeast
  (or 2 cakes compressed yeast)

¼ cup very warm water
2 eggs, beaten
1 teaspoon lemon rind,
  grated
5 cups regular flour, sifted
1 cup blanched almonds,
  chopped
¼ teaspoon nutmeg
2 tablespoons cinnamon-
  sugar

Combine raisins, candied fruits, and orange juice in a small bowl. Scald milk with sugar, salt, and ½ cup (1 stick) of the butter or margarine; cool to lukewarm. Sprinkle or crumble yeast into very warm water in a large bowl. ("Very warm" water should feel comfortably warm when dropped on wrist.) Stir until yeast dissolves, then stir in cooled milk mixture, eggs, and lemon rind. Beat in 2 cups of the flour until smooth; stir in fruit mixture, almonds, and nutmeg, then beat in just enough of remaining 3 cups of flour to make a stiff dough. Knead until smooth and elastic on a lightly floured pastry cloth or board, adding only enough flour to keep dough from sticking. Place in a large, greased bowl; cover with a clean towel. Let rise in a warm place, away from draft, 2 hours, or until double in bulk. Punch dough down; knead a few times; divide in half. Roll each into an oval, 15″ x 9″. Place on a greased, large cookie sheet. Melt remaining ½ cup (1 stick) butter or margarine in a small saucepan; brush part over each oval; sprinkle with cinnamon-sugar; fold in half lengthwise. Cover; let rise again 1 hour, or until double in bulk. Brush again with part of the remaining melted butter or margarine. Bake in moderate oven (350 degrees), for 35 minutes, or until golden brown and loaves give a hollow sound when tapped. While hot, brush with remaining melted butter or margarine; cool on wire racks.

Makes 2 large loaves   —*Family Circle,* December, 1965

After Florence left, she opened a tearoom and offered this orange bread. It is delicious toasted and served with cream cheese.

Sister Florence Phelps' Orange Bread

¼ cup butter or margarine,
   room temperature
1 cup sugar
1 egg
1 cup marmalade (store
   bought is not as good;
   directions for making
   marmalade follow)

3 cups flour
2 teaspoons baking powder
1 teaspoon salt
½ teaspoon orange extract
¾ cup milk

If making marmalade for this recipe, make marmalade first (see below). Preheat oven to 350 degrees. Cream butter and sugar. Add egg. Beat well. Stir in marmalade. Sift together flour, baking powder, salt. Add alternately with milk to creamed mixture, stirring well. Add extract. Put into 2 loaf pans (8½″ x 4½″ and 5¾″ x 3″), greased and lined with wax paper. It should be a rather limber batter. Bake 30–35 minutes. Test with a straw to determine if done. Cool on rack.

Makes 2 loaves

Marmalade for Orange Bread

Rind of 2 oranges with pith removed
1 cup salted water
¾ cup sugar

Cut rind into fine strips and put through coarse grinder. Boil rind in salted water until tender, about 15 minutes. Drain. Boil again in ¾ cup water and ¾ cup sugar. Cook until clear. It should be a thin marmalade. Cool completely and add to prepared batter.

—Bertha Lindsay's scrapbook

Rye and Whole-wheat Bread

3 tablespoons sugar
2 yeast cakes
3 cups water, warm
¼ cup vegetable oil
2 teaspoons cardamon, ground

4 cups white flour
1½ cups dry milk powder
1 tablespoon salt
2 cups rye flour
2 cups whole-wheat flour

Add sugar and yeast to 1 cup water. Let stand 10 minutes to proof. Add remaining water, oil, and cardamon. Sift in white flour, dry milk powder, and salt. Beat well for 2 minutes. Gradually add rye and whole-wheat flour, kneading as you add. Knead 10 minutes on floured board. Let rise one hour. Poke down. Turn over; rise for 45 minutes. Shape into 2 loaves and place in buttered 9″ x 5″ loaf pans. Rise. Bake at 350 degrees about 45 minutes.

—Bertha Lindsay's scrapbook

Brown bread was sold with the baked beans and pickles in the 1930s and 1940s.

Sister Aida Elam's Brown Bread

1 cup rye flour
1 cup cornmeal (Indian meal)
1 cup whole-wheat flour
1 teaspoon salt
¼ cup fine flour

1¾ cup sour milk
2 tablespoons butter or margarine, melted
¾ cup molasses
raisins (optional)

Prepare and bring to boil water in steaming kettle. Mix all dry ingredients well together in bowl. In small bowl, stir together milk, butter, and molasses. (Raisins may be added.) Add to dry ingredients and mix well. Put mixture in 2 1-pound coffee cans, 4 soup cans, or a mold. Containers should be greased well. Fill not more than ⅔ full. Cover tightly with foil. Tie on with string. Steam on rack in kettle of boiling water, 3 hours for large can, 2 hours for soup can. Remove; cool on rack.

—Notes, Shaker Archives, SVI

White Doughnuts

2 pounds bread flour
¼ cup sugar
Pinch of salt

½ cup shortening, melted
1 yeast cake
1 pint scalded milk

Knead thoroughly; let rise. Cut into 6″ lengths by 1″. Let rise until light. Fry in deep fat. Serve with maple syrup.

—*Shaker Tested Recipes*

Sister Eunice Clarke's Excellent Doughnuts

1 cup sugar
1 cup milk
2 eggs, beaten
1 teaspoon butter, melted
3½ cups flour

2 teaspoons baking powder
1 teaspoon baking soda
½ teaspoon salt
½ teaspoon nutmeg
Cinnamon (optional)

Heat at least 2″ fat in a heavy kettle. Stir together milk, sugar, eggs, and butter. Sift dry ingredients. Gradually add to milk mixture, beating well to a stiff dough. Roll out on a lightly floured board, ½″ to ⅝″ thick. Cut with doughnut cutter. Fry in hot fat (375 degrees) until golden brown, turning only once. Drain on brown paper. (1 teaspoon cinnamon may be added, or warm doughnuts may be shaken in a bag of cinnamon-sugar.)

—Notes, Shaker Archives, SVI

Puddings and Desserts[1]

"About the nicest morsel that ever tickled the palate is a boiled apple."

—Mary Whitcher's
Shaker House-Keeper

*E*veryone likes a dessert to top off a meal. Desserts should be planned so that they complement the main course. I was taught many years ago that if I was serving beef, lamb, chicken, or veal, steamed puddings of any kind follow very nicely. The Steamed Chocolate Pudding is one example, and a hard sauce or a fruit sauce can be served with it. The Fruit Rice Bavarian and the Rice Pineapple Dainty go well with stews.

Back in the early 1900s, and up into the 1930s, the Canterbury Shakers had the same organization as in the earlier years. We still had Eldresses, Elders, Deaconesses, and Deacons to oversee the various responsibilities of home. It was the Kitchen Deaconess' place to order such commodities as flour and sugar and various other items that we had to have on hand. She had keys for the cupboards where the canned goods were kept, and whatever was bought extra would be given to the cooks when they asked for it. In those years, the sugar, flour, and so forth were packed in barrels for restaurants and heavy users of these commodities. So, the

Kitchen Deaconess had a store in the west side of the North Shop[2] where a hogshead of New Orleans molasses was kept. In a room that had a dry atmosphere were the sugar, flour, and dried beans. There was also a barrel of dried Irish moss. The Irish moss was used for various purposes such as medicine and as a starch for clothing. We used it many times to stiffen antimacassars, crocheted doilies, scarves for bureaus and such, and for fine linens. Now, the Irish moss was free to the cooks to help themselves whenever they wished to make a delicious pudding called "blancmange." (This pudding was also made with cornstarch or gelatin in the World, but the Canterbury Shakers preferred the Irish moss for this delicious dessert.)[3] I don't know where the Shakers first got the Irish moss, but later, we got it dried from Barrington, New Hampshire. We now get it from Sandwich, Massachusetts. Irish moss is a fine seaweed and comes from the deep ocean. This is the recipe for the Blancmange as used here at Canterbury.

Blancmange

½ *teaspoon baking soda*
¼ *cup Irish moss, firmly*
   packed
2½ *cups milk, cold*
½ *cup sugar, or more*

1 *teaspoon vanilla*
Cream
1 *cup raspberries or*
   strawberries (optional)

Mix the baking soda with enough water to cover the Irish moss. In the soda water, wash the Irish moss, taking out all the black stems and any foreign substances, such as stones or small seashells that became lodged in it. The soda water takes out all the sand and grit. Then wash the moss in cold water to further remove the sand and taste of the soda water. I do this second step twice. The moss is then placed in the cold milk and put in a double boiler to gently boil it for at least an hour and a half. To tell when done, take a spoonful and put it on a saucer where it should quickly congeal. If not boiled long enough, continue cooking without stirring. When the mixture is done, and ready to take off the stove, add the sugar and vanilla, stirring gently until the sugar is dissolved. Put the mixture through a sieve (I use a sieve, although they used cheesecloth), and pour directly into your serving dish. The pudding must not be stirred again and can be placed in the refrigerator to cool. This pudding is served with cream, or, in the season of raspberries and strawberries, a good cup of berries can be placed in the cream to be served over the dessert.

Serves 6   *—Pictorial Review Standard Cookbook*

Steamed Chocolate Pudding

1½ cups sugar   *2½ cups flour*
⅔ cup butter   *6 teaspoons cocoa*
3 eggs   *1 teaspoon salt*
1 teaspoon vanilla   *1½ cups milk*
3½ teaspoons baking powder

Cream sugar and butter. Beat eggs and add one at a time. Add vanilla. Sift dry ingredients together and add alternately to creamed mixture with milk. Place in 2 oiled pudding tins or cleaned, oiled coffee cans, filling to just over half full. Cover tightly. Put in a large pot with 1 inch of water. Cover. Steam one hour. Serve with hard sauce. (See page 60.)

Serves 8   *—Shaker Tested Recipes*

Fruit Rice Bavarian

1 level tablespoon gelatin
½ cup cold water
1 cup cooked rice, hot
¼ cup sugar
¼ teaspoon salt

½ teaspoon vanilla
½ cup fruit
1 cup heavy cream, whipped
Nutmeats (optional)

Soak gelatin in cold water about 5 minutes and dissolve over hot water. Add to rice. Add sugar, salt, and vanilla. Beat well and mix in fruit. Fold in whipped cream. Turn into wet mold and chill. Garnish with fruit or nutmeats.

Serves 10

—Shaker Tested Recipes

Rice Pineapple Dainty

½ cup rice
½ cup finely cut pineapple, canned

⅓ cup sugar
½ cup cream, whipped stiff

Cook and blanch rice, so each grain is separate. Mix the rice, pineapple, and sugar. Fold in the cream. Serve in sherbet glasses.

Serves 4

—Shaker Tested Recipes

Spanish Cream

2 packages gelatin
2½ cups milk, cold
3 eggs, separated

½ cup sugar
Pinch salt
1 teaspoon vanilla

Dissolve gelatin in milk and let sit 5 minutes. Scald milk

and add egg yolks, which have been beaten with sugar and salt. Cook in a double boiler, stirring occasionally, until mixture thickens and coats the spoon. Fold in stiffly beaten egg whites and vanilla. Mold and chill. Spanish Cream made this way will separate into three layers. If a cream the same consistency throughout is preferred, do not add the egg whites until the custard mixture has cooled and is just ready to stiffen.

Serves 6   —*Pictorial Review Standard Cookbook*

Apricot Pudding

3 tablespoons tapioca	*1 #2 can apricots (or dried*
¼ cup white sugar	*apricots soaked in 2*
¼ teaspoon salt	*quarts water)*
¼ teaspoon cinnamon	*2 eggs, separated*
¼ teaspoon nutmeg	*2 tablespoons sugar*

Soak tapioca in 3 tablespoons water for 1 hour (unless using quick tapioca). Mix tapioca with sugar and spices. Drain juice from canned apricots and add 2 cups to mixture. Beat egg yolks and add to mixture and cook in double boiler 15 minutes. Reserve 8 apricot halves for decoration and chop remainder and fold into mixture. Pour into 2-quart casserole dish and cover with meringue. To make meringue, beat egg whites and 2 tablespoons sugar until peaks form. Bake pudding at 350 degrees for 20 minutes. After baking, garnish with apricot halves.

Serves 8–10   —Bertha Lindsay's scrapbook

Grape Sponge Pudding

½ cup sugar
5 tablespoons cornstarch
½ teaspoon salt

1 cup water
2 cups grape juice
4 egg whites, stiffly beaten

Dissolve sugar, cornstarch, and salt in the water. Put grape juice in a pan and add cornstarch mixture. Cook, stirring constantly, until pudding is thickened and rather clear. Remove from heat. Gradually fold pudding mixture into whites, until they are incorporated. Serve chilled in sherbet dishes, or chill overnight in a mold. Put molded pudding in a deep dish and pour Custard Sauce (see page 59) around pudding.

Serves 8   *—Shaker Tested Recipes*

Sister Eunice Clarke's Baked Indian Pudding

1 quart milk, scalded
⅓ cup cornmeal
1 cup molasses
2 eggs, beaten
1 teaspoon salt

2 tablespoons butter
¼ teaspoon cinnamon
½ teaspoon ginger
1 cup cold milk

Put milk in top of double boiler over simmering water. Add cornmeal slowly, stirring constantly. Cook for 15 minutes. Add molasses, butter, eggs, and spices. (Mix some hot cornmeal into eggs before adding to prevent curdling of eggs.) Turn all into oiled or buttered deep casserole dish. Pour cold milk over carefully. Do not stir or cover. Put dish into a larger, open pan of hot water.

Bake at 300 degrees for 1 hour. Lower heat to 275 degrees. Bake 4 hours. Serve warm.

Serves 10   —Notes, Shaker Archives, SVI

1938 Bertha Lindsay   L

Bread Wisdom.

In baking bread, the most important point to consider is the yeast. Keep your yeast with care. Whenever possible keep it in an ice box, where it will be dry and cold. Though yeast may discolor at times this in no ways impairs its quality. As long as it is firm it is good to use. When it becomes too soft to handle, do not use it.

The mixing.

Measure the liquid into a bowl and add the sugar. Sugar assists fermentation. Next crumble yeast into mixture. Allow to stand from six to eight minutes, add the shortening, and sift in enough flour to form a smooth light batter. Beat this thoroughly, so that the yeast may be well distributed. Salt may be dissolved or used dry.

The Kneading.

The dough must not be chilled, therefore knead quickly and lightly until it is smooth and elastic and does not stick to fingers or board.

The Rising.

After kneading place dough in a bowl and set in warm place, free from draught. Cover bowl to prevent crust forming on dough, which would cause a streak in the bread. Let the dough rise double in bulk.

The Moulding.

Next mould bread into loaves about half size of pans. Put each loaf in a well greased pan and let rise again in warm place, free from draught till double in size. To test if loaf is ready for oven, flour the finger and make an impression in loaf, if it disappears, give a little more time, if it remains bread is ready to bake.

Plate 25.   A sample of the manuscript form in which many of the Shaker recipes were recorded. ("Bread Wisdom" corresponds to pages 64–65.)

This was made long before my day by the Canterbury Shakers.

Sister Lucy Shepard's Troy Pudding

1 tablespoon butter, soft
1 cup molasses
3 cups flour
1 teaspoon baking soda
1 teaspoon cinnamon

1 teaspoon nutmeg
½ teaspoon ginger
¼ teaspoon cloves
1 cup sour milk
1 cup raisins

In large bowl, stir together butter and molasses. Sift together flour, baking soda, and spices. Add to molasses mixture, in small amounts, alternately with sour milk. Add raisins last. Mix well. Pour into an oiled pudding mold or 3 coffee cans, just over half full. Cover securely with foil that is greased where it will touch the pudding top. Place on a rack in a deep kettle on top of the stove. Fill the kettle with at least 1 inch of water, cover, and bring to boil. Reduce heat and steam for 3 hours. Check occasionally to maintain water level. Serve with hard sauce (see page 60).

Serves 12   —*Shaker Tested Recipes*

Shaker Boiled Apples

6 Baldwin apples, medium
    to large size, peeled, cored
    and sliced
½ cup sugar

Place a layer of fair-skinned Baldwins, or any nice variety, in the stewpan, with about a quarter on an inch of water. Throw on about ½ cup sugar to 6 good-sized apples, and boil until the apples are thoroughly cooked and the syrup nearly thick enough for jelly. Bring to a boil, lower heat, and simmer. Can be served with cream.

Serves 6 —Mary Whitcher, *Shaker House-Keeper*

Plate 26. Apple-picking season, October, 1918. Ethel Hudson *(third from left)*, Edith Green *(center, front row)*, Bertha Lindsay *(seated, far right)*, Florence Phelps *(standing). Shaker Archives, 1–PN112, SVI.*

The amount of work in the harvesting and preserving of the fruit was enormous. On November 7, 1900, Jessie Evans recorded: "This evening occurred the thirty-second apple cutting, closing the season. Total for drying, 1,112 bushels. After drying, 193 bushels. Entire apple harvest, 1,740 bushels." Seven years later, she wrote that the Canterbury Shakers were presented with a gasoline powered machine to pare and core the apples. In her estimation, it "proved to be a 'good labor saver.' "

Pies[1]

"Cora Helena Sarle, Mildred, and Martha . . . make three hundred hand pies which Elder Arthur has made for the school at Enfield, New Hampshire."

—Josephine E. Wilson,
diary entry, September 16, 1935

By the time I was thirteen years of age, I was given the responsibility of making the pies in the bake room of the Dwelling House. In those days, the Shakers had pies for breakfast, dinner, and supper. We had boys and Brothers who worked hard early in the morning, milking the cows and taking care of the Horse Barn and the Cow Barn, and so they wanted a good, big breakfast when they were through. I guess it was the way of other people elsewhere to have pie for breakfast, too. So, I learned to make twenty-six pies on a Saturday, to last over to Sunday.

I've had to change my crust-making ways over time. I used to use lard, and then we weren't supposed to use animal fat, so I use Crisco now. I use two cups of flour, a scant cup of Crisco, and a little salt. Sometimes I use orange juice, sometimes I use water, but if I have buttermilk, I use that. When we were making pie crust for the Family, we had to use a large amount. We had the flour all measured out, and we heated the lard, just enough. The buttermilk was cold. We mixed it all up with the salt. When the War came, we used part lard and part beef fat; I don't remember the proportion, but we had a little more lard than beef—it hardens, you know. And we still had the buttermilk. I made the crust the night before and left it out so that it was ready to roll in the morning. I know the cookbooks say to have it cold, right from the refrigerator, but I can't manage it. I never went by the cookbooks, I went by what I learned from the older Sisters.

I save the leftover crust and freeze it for the next pie. If I don't want to put it away, I make "pockets" out of it, or "snails," but I don't have little girls to make them for anymore. You roll it out as thin or as thick as you want. Add butter, sugar, and cinnamon and roll it up and curl it around. Bake at 375 degrees until it's brown.

Apple pies were especially popular at Canterbury. Many varieties of apples were grown here: Baldwin, Rhode Island Greening, Russet, Blue Pearmain, Astrachan, Fameuse, Northern Spy, President, Pippin, MacIntosh, Canadian Red, Wealthy, and the August Sweet. We used Talman Sweets for baking in the summer and Yellow Transparents and Maiden's Blush in the spring. In the fall, we used the Jonathans for boiling. The Winesaps were also a favorite at that time of the year. The Nonesuch, Sheep's Nose, and Turkey Egg apples were used for mincemeat pies, but the Granny Smith has proved to be a favorite with me for making apple pies. It is a very good keeper. The Chenango, or Virgin apple, was a very dry apple when cooked, so we were very fond of using it when making the famous Shaker Hand Pies. The Newton Pippin and the Round Pippin were also very dry apples, so we would always use these if the Chenangos failed.

I have found that rose water gives a unique flavor to the apple pie and seems to be very popular. In the early days, the Shakers had no flavorings to use but lemon and rose water. The Shakers at Mount Lebanon, New York, raised acres of roses, especially to make rose water as a flavoring. It was used in puddings and cakes as well as apple pies. Many prefer nutmeg as a flavor. I add a dash of nutmeg and a tablespoon of rose water to two tablespoons of water and sprinkle this over the apples. According to the apple, use a half a cup to two-thirds of a cup of sugar. Do not use too much sugar— say, half a cup—to the Granny Smiths, particularly.

The following recipe was passed down to me.

Rose Water Apple Pie

> 1 2-layer pie crust, 9",
>   unbaked
> 5–7 tart apples (7, if small)
> ½ cup sugar
> Dash salt
> 1 tablespoon rose water,
>   diluted in 2 tablespoons
>   water
> Dash nutmeg
> 1 tablespoon cornstarch
> 2 teaspoons margarine

Mix ingredients.* Add to pie shell and cover with crust. Cook at 425 degrees 5–10 minutes. Turn oven to 350 degrees and cook 45 minutes.

* Today's cook may want to use more sugar (¾ cup) and less rose water (½ teaspoon to 1 tablespoon).

When I was a schoolgirl of thirteen years of age, Sister Jessie Evans, our teacher, asked the students to have a contest. The boys were to make articles of wood or to raise vegetables—anything that boys would do or were being taught. The girls would take sewing, cooking, knitting, or crocheting as their contribution. Well, my first attempt at making pies was to make a lemon meringue pie, which I did, and I won the contest! The recipe follows.

Eldress Bertha's
Lemon Meringue Pie

4 yolks, beaten
1 cup sugar
Pinch salt
3 tablespoons cornstarch
Juice of 2–3 lemons
   (according to size), cold

Juice of 1 orange, cold
1 cup boiling water
1 tablespoon (generous)
   butter
4 tablespoons sugar
1 baked 9" pie crust

Mix sugar with yolks. Add salt. Mix cornstarch with juices and add to egg mixture. Add boiling water. Cook on stove in double boiler until thick. Take off stove and add butter. Let stand while making meringue (see below). Put filling into crust, then top with meringue. The only variation I make in the lemon pie is to add the juice of 1 orange, but I make sure to keep the pie lemony. So, I put in 2 lemons, and, sometimes a little grated rind.

Meringue for Pie

3 egg whites, beaten
6 tablespoons sugar
1 teaspoon lemon juice
½ teaspoon cream of tartar

While beating whites, slowly add sugar, juice, and

cream of tartar. Meringues sometimes fall. I have found that if you heat the oven to 425, turn it off, put the pie in and bake until the meringue is dry (about 10 to 15 minutes), you will have a high, delicious meringue.

—Quoted to the editor, 1986

In this recipe I use butter cookies. I don't like them to eat, and I always get a box at Christmas, so I save them for the squash pie.

Squash Pie

2 cups butternut or winter
  squash, cooked
¼ teaspoon salt
1 cup sugar
2 eggs, beaten
2 cups milk
½–⅓ cup cracker crumbs
  (saltines) or butter cookie
  crumbs
1 teaspoon cinnamon
1 scant teaspoon ginger
9" pie shell, unbaked

Mix ingredients and add to pie shell. If the squash is very wet use less milk. Bake at 425 degrees, 12–15 minutes (to make the crust firm), then at 325 degrees, 35–40 minutes.

—Bertha Lindsay's notes,
Shaker Archives, SVI

Sometimes the Shakers would make picnic lunches that included little hand pies, sandwiches, a piece of cake, and a beverage. A hand pie made a delicious picnic dessert.

Shaker Hand Pie

Pie crust, using pastry flour
12 ounces applesauce, fresh
*   or canned*
Sugar, to taste (if using
*   canned applesauce, omit*
*   sugar)*
½ teaspoon nutmeg
Raisins

Roll pie crust and cut into 12 rounds, about 4"–5" in diameter. Season applesauce with sugar and nutmeg. Put 2 tablespoons of sauce on six rounds. Add several raisins to the sauce. Wet edge of each round, and cover bottom crusts with top crusts. Pinch edges together. Bake in a 400 degree oven for about 20 minutes.

Makes 6 small pies   *— Shaker Tested Recipes*

Maine Blueberry Pie

1 quart blueberries
1 cup sugar
¾ cup water
3½ tablespoons cornstarch
¼ teaspoon salt
¼ cup water
Dash cloves (optional)
9" pie shell, baked
Whipped cream

Reserve 3 cups berries; cook remaining berries with sugar and water. Make a paste of cornstarch, salt, and water. Add to cooked blueberries and cook until thickened. A scant amount of cloves is often good with the blueberry pie to bring out the flavor. Add hot mixture to uncooked berries and turn into pastry shell. Chill 3 hours. Top with whipped cream and serve.

—Bertha Lindsay's scrapbook

Pumpkin Pecan Pie

3 eggs, beaten
1 cup cooked, mashed
   pumpkin
1 cup sugar
½ cup corn syrup
1 cup pecans, chopped
1 teaspoon milk
1 teaspoon cinnamon
1 teaspoon (scant) salt
9" pie shell, unbaked
Whipped cream

Mix all ingredients together except for whipped cream and pie shell. Pour ingredients into fluted (open) pie shell. Bake for 12 minutes at 450 degrees, then at 350 degrees for 35 to 40 minutes. When the pie has cooled slightly, add whipped cream around the edge.

—Bertha Lindsay's notes,
Shaker Archives, SVI

Rice Pie

3 tablespoons butter or
  margarine (soft)
½ cup sugar
½ teaspoon salt (optional)
3 eggs, beaten well
1 cup rice, cooked

1½ cup milk
1 teaspoon vanilla
9" pie shell
Jelly (preferably crab apple or
  apple)
½ cup coconut

Cream butter, sugar, and salt. Add eggs and mix well. Add rice, milk, and vanilla. Mix together well. Pour into pie shell. Bake like custard. Bake 15 minutes at 450 degrees, then reduce heat to 350 degrees and continue baking for 20–25 minutes. After removing from oven, cover top with very thin slices or teaspoons of jelly, then sprinkle with coconut.

— Shaker Tested Recipes

This recipe was passed down to me. I put a lattice crust or a whole crust on top.

Strawberry Rhubarb Pie

1 cup (generous) rhubarb,
  cut up
1 cup (generous)
  strawberries, sliced
Pinch salt
1 cup sugar

2 tablespoons (generous)
  cornstarch or tapioca
Butter (or margarine)
Unbaked pie shell (additional
  crust for top optional)

Mix rhubarb, berries, and salt. Mix sugar and cornstarch and add to berries. Put in pie shell. Dot with butter. Bake raw in the oven at 400 degrees to start, for 10 minutes, until the crust sets. Turn the oven down to 375 degrees and cook until done, about 45 minutes.

Funny Cake

1 ¼ cup cake flour
1 teaspoon baking powder
½ teaspoon salt
¾ cup sugar
¼ cup shortening
½ cup milk
1 teaspoon vanilla
1 egg, unbeaten
3 tablespoons nuts or coconut

Measure dry ingredients into sifter. Place shortening in bowl. Sift in dry ingredients. Add milk and vanilla. Mix until all flour is moistened. Beat well. Add egg. Beat. Pour into pie plate. Pour lukewarm sauce (see below) over batter. Sprinkle with nuts or coconut. Bake in oven 350 degrees for 50 to 55 minutes. Serve warm.

Butterscotch Sauce for Funny Cake

¼ cup butter
½ cup brown sugar, firmly
  packed
2 tablespoons corn syrup
3 tablespoons water
½ teaspoon vanilla

Combine first three ingredients. Cook, stirring over low heat to boiling point. Add water. Boil again. Stir in vanilla.

—Bertha Lindsay's scrapbook

Plate 27. Canterbury Shakers and young residents, Dwelling House, ministry dining room, c. 1920. Aida Elam *(far left),* Evelyn Polsey *(second from left),* Frida Weeks *(center),* Miriam Wall *(third from right),* Ida Crook *(second from right). Shaker Archives, 11–P265, SVI.*

The ministry dining room was originally built for the Elders and Eldresses to use, but as the numbers of Shakers—and particularly Brethren—decreased, its initial function ceased to be necessary. By the 1900s, the Shakers, primarily Elder Arthur Bruce and his friends, used the room for special occasions. The reason for this gathering is unknown, but the Sisters and young residents pictured here were probably celebrating a birthday party.

Cakes[1]

"Easter Sunday. Aida is in the kitchen, and she and Helena arranged a dainty dish of colored eggs for breakfast and serve angel cake and 'bunnies' with many other pretty dishes for dinner. An Easter program of one hour is given in [the] evening. Very beautiful and well rendered."

—Josephine E. Wilson,
diary entry, April 21, 1935

Who doesn't like to make cakes? I think they are one of the most fascinating dishes that you can make. There are so many recipes and all so good. I approve of the package mixes for those who do not cook very much or do not have time to cook, but for homemakers who love to cook, cakes made from scratch can never be beat.

When I started learning how to make cakes, I was already a proficient cook. No one had to teach me; I followed recipes. At that time one of the hired men, who had two daughters, was living at our upper North Family, and we provided desserts for them every week. That is when I first learned to make cakes.

Many of our holidays were recognized by a fancier meal than the everyday one. Cooks could use their culinary artistry in any form that they wished in preparing a pretty meal, according to the occasion. (See plate 27.) We rarely had birthday cakes for our people, but, in later days, we made cakes for each other and for friends.[2] I once made an oval birthday cake for Sister Lillian Phelps, and I decorated it with flowers. Elder Arthur came down the stairs to the kitchen when I was fixing the roses and said I was very extravagant! I made two other cakes for Lillian; one when she was ninety and one when she was ninety-seven.

Sister Miriam Wall was a very good cook and particularly liked to bake cakes. Miriam made the cloaks at Canterbury and worked with Eldress Mary Wilson. Sister Miriam was about a year or two older than me. She had her turn in the kitchen as we all did. Mildred used to say, "Miriam is a very good cook, and Bertha is a fancy cook."[3] I used to like to add garnishes and cut things out, like baskets out of oranges. The baskets had a handle cut out of them. I filled them with dates and coconut and baked them to just warm. We had them at Easter.

The following recipe was also made at Easter. It was started long before my time. I picked it up from the older Sisters.

Calla Lilies

5 eggs
5 tablespoons water
1 cup sugar
1 teaspoon vanilla
2 teaspoons baking powder
1 cup flour
1 tablespoon butter, melted
(additional butter, sugar,
    and yellow food coloring
    for icing "stamens")

Beat eggs until light and frothy. Add water, sugar, and vanilla. Beat well. Sift baking powder with flour, then sift into wet mixture and mix well. Add butter last. Butter an oven-proof saucer for each "lily." Spoon 2 tablespoons batter into each saucer. Bake at 350 degrees for 10 minutes or until pale gold, not brown. Fold bottom ends over to make a funnel. Secure each with toothpicks. Make icing "stamens." Roll icing mixture (butter, sugar, and yellow food coloring) into thin stems and insert into funnel of "lily." Calla Lilies may be either iced white or covered with a coat of whipped cream. This pastry is pretty enough to be served at any special occasion.

Makes 12–15 "Lilies"

～

Sister Miriam and I both used to love to make Golden Angel Cake for the Family. We were very fond of making it because when you make regular angel cake, you have all those yolks left over. So, we made the Golden Angel Cake to take care of all of those yolks.

Sister Miriam Wall's Golden Angel Cake

1½ cups sugar
4 eggs, separated
1 tablespoon water
1 teaspoon vanilla
1½ cups flour
½ teaspoon cream of tarter
½ cup boiling water

Beat sugar, yolks, 1 tablespoon water, and vanilla for 10 minutes. Sift flour and cream of tartar and add with boiling water to egg mixture. Fold in beaten egg whites. Bake 1 hour in ungreased tube pan in oven at 350 degrees.

—Bertha Lindsay's scrapbook;
also in *Shaker Tested Recipes*

～

The Golden Angel or any kind of angel cake can be used for the following recipe. I use an instant mix now, which is easier for me. Split the baked and cooled angel cake in half and add filling. Let set before serving.

Bavarian Filling

2 cups milk
1 tablespoon gelatin
½ cup sugar
4 egg yolks, slightly beaten

⅛ teaspoon salt
1 tablespoon sugar
¾ teaspoon vanilla
1 cup heavy cream, beaten

Scald 1¾ cups milk. Sprinkle gelatin over rest of cold milk (¼ cup). Caramelize ½ cup sugar and add carefully to scalded milk. Combine yolks with salt and 1 tablespoon sugar. Pour scalded milk over egg mixture and return to heat until thick. Add gelatin mixture, stir, cool, and add vanilla. Chill until thick. Fold in cream.

—Notes, Shaker Archives, SVI

The following is a recipe for an old-fashioned coffee cake. The recipe was given to me by June Sprigg, who used to visit the Moravian Village in Bethlehem, Pennsylvania.

Moravian Sugar Cake

1 yeast cake, dissolved in ½ cup warm water
2 cups whole milk
1 cup potatoes, cooked and mashed
1 teaspoon salt
3–5 cups flour

½ cup butter
½ cup lard
1–2 eggs, well beaten
1 cup white sugar
Lumps of butter
Brown sugar
Cinnamon

Dissolve yeast in water. Mix milk, potatoes, salt, and yeast. Add sufficient flour to make a stiff sponge. Beat well and put in a warm place until very light (approximately doubles, 1–2 hours). Melt butter and lard together. Add eggs and sugar. Add a little more flour and work the sponge until blisters form and dough drops clean from the hand. Spread dough to ½ inch thickness in 2–3 greased pans. Let rise. When cake is light, make holes in equal distances, filling each with a lump of butter and brown sugar. Sprinkle plenty of brown sugar and some cinnamon over entire cake. Bake in moderate oven, 350 degrees, for approximately 20 minutes.

The cake from this recipe is not very sweet and can be served as a side dish.

Blueberry Cake

½ cup shortening   Dash of nutmeg
¾ cup sugar   2 teaspoons baking powder
1 egg, well beaten   1 cup (scant) milk
Pinch salt   1 cup blueberries (fresh or
2 cups flour   frozen)
Dash of cinnamon

Cream shortening and sugar. Add egg. Sift dry ingredients together and add, alternately with milk, to egg mixture. Fold in the blueberries. (Frozen, unsweetened blueberries may be used, but thaw them, drain well, pat dry with a paper towel, and lightly flour.) Put in a greased baking pan and bake at 400 degrees for 40–45 minutes in a 9″ x 9″ pan.

—Bertha Lindsay's scrapbook
(newspaper clipping from Mrs. Edgar
Ingersow, Hampton, New Hampshire)

This cake is very moist. Be sure to drain the zucchini, and don't grate it too fine.

Chocolate Zucchini Cake

1 cup brown sugar
½ cup white sugar
½ cup butter
½ cup oil
3 eggs
1 teaspoon vanilla
½ cup buttermilk
2½ cups flour

½ teaspoon allspice
½ teaspoon cinnamon
½ teaspoon salt
2 teaspoons baking soda
4 tablespoons cocoa
2½ cups zucchini, grated, drained well
½–1 cup chocolate chips

Cream sugars, butter, and oil together. Add eggs, vanilla, and buttermilk. Mix well. Measure dry ingredients and sift into mixture. Add zucchini. Mix until well blended. Pour into greased and floured 9″ x 13″ pan. Sprinkle chocolate chips on top. Bake at 325 degrees for 45 minutes to 1 hour or until done.

—Nola Stokes, 1980

Shaker Apple Cake

1 cup dried apples (or apricots)	1¾ cups flour, sifted
1 cup molasses	2 teaspoons baking soda
⅔ cup sour cream	1 teaspoon cinnamon
1 cup sugar	½ teaspoon cloves
1 egg	½ teaspoon salt

Soak dried apples overnight. In the morning, cut fine and simmer in molasses for 20 minutes. Cool. Combine sour cream, sugar, and egg. Beat until smooth. Combine dry ingredients and sift several times. Blend both mixtures and beat until smooth. Add fruit and molasses and turn into buttered loaf pan. Bake in moderate, 350-degree oven for 1 hour.

—Notes, Shaker Archives, SVI

The following recipe came from *Woman's Day* or *Family Circle*. I wanted to try it because it is unusual. (Everyone knows about Carrot Cake.) It is best to serve in the summer when the tomatoes are good.

Fresh Tomato Cake

1 cup dark brown sugar	3 cups flour, sifted
½ cup shortening	2 teaspoons baking powder
2 eggs	1 teaspoon baking soda
½ cup nuts, chopped	1 teaspoon nutmeg
½ cup dates, chopped	½ teaspoon salt
½ cup raisins	
2 cups tomatoes, peeled and cubed	

Cream sugar and shortening. Add eggs, nuts, dates, raisins, and tomatoes. Sift dry ingredients into tomato mixture. Pour into greased and floured 9″ x 13″ pan. Bake at 350 degrees for 30 minutes. Cool and add frosting.

Frosting for Tomato Cake

8 ounces cream cheese
1½ cups confectioners sugar
3 tablespoons butter
1 teaspoon vanilla
1⅛ teaspoons salt

Beat ingredients with electric mixer until smooth. Frost cooled cake.

—Bertha Lindsay's scrapbook

The following was passed down from Sister Lucy Ann Shepard. It was also a favorite of Leona Merrill Rowell's.

Sister Lucy Ann Shepard's Fruitcake

2 cups butter, scant   2 teaspoons allspice
2 cups sugar   2 cups citron
12 eggs   2 cups currants
2½ cups flour   ½ pint brandy
2 teaspoons cinnamon

Soften butter. Add sugar, eggs, and beat well. Add dry ingredients sifted together. Add fruit and brandy. Mix thoroughly and bake 1 hour in slow oven.

Makes 2 loaves   —*Gourmet's Delight*

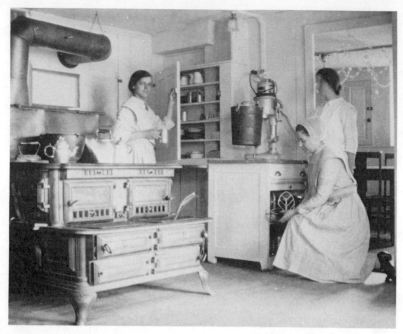

Plate 29.   Preparing to make ice cream, Dwelling House kitchen, Messer's corner, 1926. Gertrude Roberts *(left)*, Evelyn Polsey *(center). Shaker Archives, PN237, SVI.*

In January, 1926, the Canterbury Brethren bought a used Kitchen Aid appliance and the cabinet in which to store it from the A. Perley Fitch Company, a drugstore in Concord. The labor-saving device was well received. At Christmas that year, one Sister composed a poem about it:

> *When we cooks now play the Kitchen Aid,*
> *All the grinders, sieves, and fancy beaters*
> *Have been relegated to the shelf,*
> *For we simply touch a little lever,*
> *And the ice cream will make itself.*

Cookies[1]

"About a month ago the Shaker Family at Canterbury packed an immense box with many kinds of goodies, from ginger snaps to maple sugar, and sent it to the embarkation hospital of the American Red Cross at Newport News, Virginia. . . . In the afternoon at the camps the Colonel complained because his light was shut off by the big box in front of his office, and all hands took hold and unpacked it in the open. When the Colonel complained again, peace was made by a ginger snap out of a package which had broken from its fastenings. . . . We distributed the goodies among the men who had just come across the sea."

—Capt. W. Irving Blanchard, M.D.
[Found in Josephine E. Wilson's diary, February 10, 1919]

*F*or many years, Miriam, Mildred and I made cookies for Christmas gifts, just as people do in many homes elsewhere. Cookies make very acceptable gifts as homemade articles.

There is a recipe for a rose geranium cake in which the leaves are put in the bottom of the pan, and, from there, the flavor goes into the cake. I adapted this idea by pulverizing the rose geranium leaves and lemon verbena leaves for use in cookies. I think the lovely flavor of both of these plants should never be lost. Both the lemon verbena cookie flavored with lemon juice and the rose geranium cookie with the rose water have a particular taste.

The basic recipe I worked from was given to me by Virginia Dudley, when she was working in the museum sandwich shop around 1980.

Lemon Verbena Cookies

2⅓ cups flour
1 cup sugar
1 teaspoon baking soda
½ teaspoon cream of tartar
½ teaspoon salt
½ cup milk
1 teaspoon lemon juice*
  (or rose water, for rose
  geranium leaves)

⅓ cup cooking oil
1 egg, beaten
2 tablespoons lemon verbena
  (or rose geranium leaves,
  if rose water is used),
  pulverized

Sift together dry ingredients. Mix liquids and add lemon verbena. Drop by teaspoonfuls on a greased cookie sheet. Bake at 350 degrees for 12–15 minutes.

Makes 4 dozen cookies

* Lemon extract is recommended as a substitute.

⌖

   This recipe can also be used with carob morsels. I change the recipe slightly, depending on the flavoring that is used.

Carob Cookies

¾ cup white sugar
1 cup brown sugar, firmly
  packed
1 cup shortening
2 eggs
2½ cups flour, sifted

1 teaspoon baking powder
12 ounces carob morsels
½ teaspoon water
1 cup nuts, chopped
1 teaspoon vanilla

Cream sugars and shortening. Add eggs. Combine flour and baking powder. Add to sugar mixture. Add remaining ingredients. Drop by teaspoonful onto a greased cookie sheet. Bake in 350-degree oven for 10 minutes.

Makes 6 dozen small cookies

⌐

Brownies

⅔ cup butter
2 cups sugar
4 eggs
4 squares unsweetened
   chocolate, melted and
   cooled

1½ cups flour
1 teaspoon baking powder
1 teaspoon salt
1 cup nuts, chopped

Cream butter and sugar and add eggs. Add chocolate. Combine flour, baking powder, and salt. Add dry mixture to chocolate mixture. Finally, add nuts. Pour into 9″ x 13″ pan. Bake in 350-degree oven for 20–25 minutes. Cut into squares.

—Notes, Shaker Archives, SVI

⌐

Brownie Cookies

1 cup sugar
½ cup shortening
2 eggs
2 squares unsweetened
   chocolate, melted

1 cup flour
½ teaspoon baking powder
½ teaspoon salt
½ teaspoon vanilla
1 cup nuts, chopped

Cream sugar and shortening together. Add eggs. Beat well. Add chocolate, flour, baking powder, and salt. Blend well. Add vanilla and nuts. Bake in 350-degree oven for 10 minutes.

Makes 40 cookies

—Bertha Lindsay's scrapbook

As zucchini was not grown at Canterbury until modern times, no early recipes require this vegetable. I have also found that zucchini was not as well liked as other vegetables, although it is very delicious eaten raw in a salad. Many people prefer sweets, so I like to use zucchini in cookies and cakes.

Orange Zucchini Bars

1 cup sugar
1½ cups flour, unsifted
1 teaspoon baking soda
1 teaspoon baking powder
½ teaspoon salt
1 teaspoon cinnamon
½ cup nuts, chopped

1 cup zucchini, chopped,
  grated, and drained
2 egg whites, lightly beaten
½ cup orange juice, frozen or
  fresh
4 tablespoons vegetable oil
1½ teaspoons orange peel, grated

Mix dry ingredients. Stir in nuts and zucchini. To egg whites, add juice and oil and fold into dry mixture. Add orange peel. Pour into greased and floured 9″ x 13″ pan. Bake at 350 degrees for 40–45 minutes.

—Nola Stokes, 1980

Ginger Creams

½ cup shortening
1 cup sugar
1 egg
1 cup molasses
4 cups flour
½ teaspoon salt (optional)

½–1 teaspoon nutmeg
2 teaspoons ginger
1 teaspoon cloves
1 teaspoon cinnamon
2 teaspoons baking soda
1 cup water, hot

Cream shortening and sugar. Add egg and beat well. Add molasses. In a separate bowl, combine flour, salt, and spices. Dissolve soda in hot water and add alternately with spice mixture to shortening mixture. Chill dough. Drop by teaspoonfuls on greased cookie sheet. Bake in 350-degree oven 10 minutes. While still warm, cover with thin icing (see below). (Cookies are also nice without icing.)

Icing for Ginger Creams

2 cups confectioners sugar   1 tablespoon butter, melted
3–4 tablespoons cream   1 teaspoon vanilla

Combine above ingredients and cover ginger creams.

Makes 6 dozen   —Bertha Lindsay's *Geography,* post 1938
                               (first appeared in the *Boston Globe*)

Filled Cookies

½ cup shortening   ¼ teaspoon baking soda
1 cup sugar   ½ teaspoon salt
2 eggs   Apricot jam (or strawberry
1 teaspoon vanilla   jam or marmalade)
2½ cups flour

Mix shortening, sugar, and eggs thoroughly. Stir in vanilla. In a separate bowl, stir dry ingredients together and add to egg mixture. Chill dough. Roll dough 1/16" thick on floured board. Cut with round cutter 2½" in diameter. Cut 2 rounds for each cookie. Place bottom pieces on lightly greased baking sheet. Spread a teaspoonful of apricot jam on each. Cover with top round. Press edges together with floured tines of fork or fingertip. Bake in 350-degree oven 8–10 minutes until delicately browned.

Makes 4½ dozen   —Bertha Lindsay's notes; possibly
                               from *Better Homes and Gardens*

Peanut Butter Cookies

1 cup brown sugar   *1 cup peanut butter*
1 cup white sugar   *2 cups flour*
1 cup butter   *1 level teaspoon baking soda*
2 eggs   *¼ teaspoon salt*

Combine ingredients and chill dough. Drop from teaspoon and press with tines of fork onto ungreased baking sheet. (The tines leave a ribbed top on each cookie.) Bake in 350-degree oven for 8–10 minutes.

Makes more than 100   *—Shaker Tested Recipes*

Confections[1]

*"Have bought three crates of oranges (eighty count) and
three crates of grapefruit (forty-six count) for sugaring."*

—Josephine E. Wilson,
diary entry, January 25, 1922

*F*or many years, the sugaring of nuts, flag root, grapefruit
peel, and orange peel was done at the village. Quite a few
butternut trees used to grow around here. In the early days,
and right up until the 1950s, the nuts were sugared and sold
as confections. These were delicious in cakes, too, and just
for plain eating. I don't know of very many butternut trees
left in the village at the present time.

The Shakers used to make confections for the gift shop
because the public was very fond of them. Sister Amy Sargent
was in charge of this work, and we used to help her package
them in small boxes for sale. But she passed away at an early
age, and Sister Rebecca took over the trade. We then helped
her from the beginning, taking the peel from the fruit,
through the sugaring process, to the packaging. And these
were very tasty confections in those days! After Sister Rebecca
gave up this work, it was passed to me, when I was in my
thirties or forties, and I enjoyed doing it so very much. I was
particularly fond of working with the flag root and the maple
sugar cakes.

The Shakers claimed that flag root[2] was very good for stomach troubles. It must be dug up in the spring, because it is then easier to scrape and cut. For many years, the Shakers cut the flag by hand. When electricity came to Canterbury, Brother Irving took an old sewing machine and fitted it with knives. We used it to cut the flag root quite thin, and the machine alleviated our work.

After the flag root was finished cooking and was sugared, there was always syrup left over with little pieces of flag in it. I used to take this syrup and make it into fudge, which was also well liked. The syrup, of course, preserved all of the leftover ingredients, which was helpful, as we were instructed not to waste anything.

There were more than one thousand maples at Maple Grove, or the East Farm,[3] as it was also called, where the sugar making was done in the very early days. Thousands of pounds of maple products were made in a good year. I think it is recorded that one year the Canterbury Shakers made more than four thousand pounds of maple products, including maple syrup and maple candy.[4] The candy was made like taffy. This was cooked to a certain degree until it was spun from the spoon when you took it up a little. It was then poured onto marble, where it was worked until it became easy to handle. From there it was pulled on a hook, back and forth, until it commenced to harden and was quite cool. The candy was then cut into six-inch lengths. The maple cakes were also popular. The talk of the village at that season was always that the St. Paul's schoolboys would come over, about forty of them, just to buy the maple sugar cakes and candy.[5]

Through the years, the Shakers also raised bees, producing honey for the table and to sell. Elder Henry was perhaps the most noted of all the beekeepers. Much later, Sister Alice Howland took over this work. Honey is versatile and very tasty and can be used in cooking. So, honey and maple syrup added much to the different dishes we made.

We also made many varieties of candy for our own pleasure, not just for sale, such as divinity fudge, penuche, and taffy. And, if you know young people, they always want

Plate 30. Picnic at the Meeting House Lane, c. 1924. Cora Helena Sarle *(left),* Miriam Wall *(far right). Shaker Archives, 1–PN83, SVI.*

candy. So, we could make any kind they wanted, under the direction of Sister Helena and Sister Rebecca, who were very kind in helping out. And then, too, we had popcorn ball parties! Making the popcorn balls was always one of the greatest pleasures of the year, because the corn could be popped over the nice, hot coals up in our ironing room and down in the washroom in the Laundry. A machine was designed by the Shakers to form the popcorn balls. The device was made from scratch, with a tin plate and two cups. We cooked New Orleans molasses, which was very light, until it spun a thread, and poured it over the popcorn. We had to work quickly because the molasses hardens. Molasses in the popcorn balls was the thing! And each of us always wanted to be the one to make the popcorn balls. (Well, we didn't fight for the chance to make them, but we sort of nudged each other to find out who wanted to be the one.)

Whenever we had a popcorn party, Sister Lillian would get up an entertainment spontaneously. One of the things she had us girls do was to get combs and have us blow into them over tissue paper, and, of course, we could sing the tune right along through them. And, when the radios first came out, she thought of the idea for us to use the combs as if we were talking over the radio, so it made a very interesting evening for everybody. (See plate 31.)

And so, we enjoyed all of these pleasures that gave us some of the little extras to eat that we found so tantalizingly good.

THE SUGARING

When the days were growing cool
Down beside a rushing pool
Oft Rebecca I have seen
In her sweater of dark green.
"I must get this flag," said she,
Just as quickly as can be.
For they ought to take some down
To the sale in Boston town.

So the roots she cut with glee
Scraped each one so agilely.
Sliced them fine on her machine
Then in milk they were boiled clean.
In the syrup let them swell
With the sugar coated well.
Then in boxes 116
At the Plaza last were seen.

—Poem written by a Sister about Sister
Rebecca Hathaway's sugared flag root.
Notebook, n.d., Shaker Archives, SVI

Candied Orange Peel

Orange rind (or grapefruit rind)
White sugar
Confectioners sugar

Peel rind from orange or grapefruit. (Find the thick-skinned fruit that can be had in the winter, usually.) Put the skins in cold sugar-water (a solution of 1 cup white sugar to 1 cup water), enough to cover. Cook slowly. Boil, drain, then change to another sugar-water solution. Cook until tender, but not broken. Slice the skins into lengths 2"–3" long and a good ¼" wide. Make a thin sugar syrup and dip. Dry overnight. Make a heavy syrup (1 cup of sugar to 1 cup of water) and dip again. We used to put the peel in crocks until spring. We would then heat and drain them and put them through the powdered sugar process. (Make a mixture of ½ powdered sugar and ½ white sugar and roll the peels in it. Repeat with a little less white sugar.)

—Quoted to the editor, 1986

Eldress Bertha's Flag Fudge

2 cups flag root syrup   *1 tablespoon butter*
½ cup (generous) sugar   *Pinch salt*
1 cup flag root (small pieces)

Boil ingredients to a soft ball stage. Stir off like any fudge.

—Rebecca Hathaway and
Bertha Lindsay's notes

Sister Rebecca Hathaway's
Sugared Flag Root

Dig and clean roots. The newer, larger roots are best. All the brown, outer skin must be removed. Then soak in cold water. Cut in thin slices and again wash. Drain well. Put into kettle and add plenty of cold water. Bring to the boiling point, then drain well and put on more cold water and bring to boiling point. Repeat this 4 or 5 times. Drain well and spread thinly on sheets to dry overnight. In the morning, divide into small lots of about 2 pounds. Make heavy syrup of 1 cup sugar to 1

Plate 31. Canterbury Shakers and friends popping corn in the Laundry wash room, c. 1922. Rebecca Hathaway *(far left)*, Lillian Phelps *(second from right). Shaker Archives, 11–P21, SVI.*

Popping corn was an inexpensive and convenient way for the Sisters to take a break while they carried on their many chores in the Laundry. The corn could be popped either on the stove in the wash room on the first floor or in the ironing room on the second floor. Posed with Sister Rebecca and Sister Lillian in this picture are probably the Percys and the Cronins, friends who visited the Shakers and proposed such a party in 1922.

cup water, and when boiling, add the flag root. Simmer gently for about 1 hour or until transparent, and syrup is nearly absorbed in the flag root. Drain and cool, then put through sugar (dry), separating each slice, then pass to next sugar dish which is ½ granulated and ½ confectioners XXXX sugar. Spread on shallow pans and dry. To dry, place outside in sunshine; this makes a whiter product. Do not pack away until well-dried, as mixture will cause it to mold.

—Rebecca Hathaway's notes

Candied Violets and Rose Leaves

Violet heads or rose leaves, dry   *½ pint water*
1 pound white sugar   *Powdered sugar*

To make the syrup, boil the sugar and water until it will form a "ball" when a little is dropped in cold water. Remove from fire. Drop selected rose leaves and violets into the syrup, pressing down without stirring. Bring syrup to a boil again and pour into a bowl and set away. The next day, drain the flowers into a fine sieve. Add ¼ pound of water to the syrup and boil again to the ball stage. Put the flowers in again. Bring to the boiling point and set away. On the third day, repeat the process, but this time when the syrup comes to a boil, wait until sugar granulates, then pour syrup and flowers onto marble, or waxed paper. Spread out to dry. Breakage can best be avoided by separating the flowers with a silver fork. Sprinkle with powdered sugar before quite dry to hold. You can pack them in a little powdered sugar.

—Notes, Shaker Archives, SVI

I was told the following recipe is two hundred years old:

Shaker Horehound Candy

3 cups boiling water
3 ounces horehound leaves
6 cups dark brown sugar
1 teaspoon cream of tartar
1 teaspoon butter
1 teaspoon lemon juice

Steep leaves 20 minutes and strain. Add sugar, cream of tartar, and butter. Cook to hard ball stage and add lemon juice. Pour into buttered pan and cut when nearly hard. (Candymakers use oil of marrubium for flavoring instead of the leaves. This oil is prepared from the plant and is available. It takes but little oil; too much will make the candy bitter.)

—Bertha Lindsay's scrapbook

Crystallized Popcorn

1 cup New Orleans molasses
(or any light molasses, or
1 tablespoon butter, 3
tablespoons water, and 1
cup sugar)
3 quarts popcorn, popped

Cook molasses or boil butter, water, and sugar until ready to candy, then pour on popcorn. Set away from the fire until partially cool. Form into balls or sticks.

—Notes, Shaker Archives, SVI

Maple Sugar Cakes

2 quarts maple syrup

Boil down the syrup until a ball can be made in ice water. Take off heat. This quantity of syrup boils down to 1 quart as a rule. Let cool. Continue stirring to make it fine grain. Continue stirring and test. (Pour a drop on marble. If it forms a "peppermint drop" and stays, it's ready.) Pour into molds that have been wet in ice water. Let cool.

—Quoted to the editor, 1986

Plate 32. Haying at Canterbury Village, c. 1924–1926. Archie Young, hired hand *(probably center)*. *Shaker Archives, 1–PN51, SVI.*

Throughout the history of the Canterbury Shakers, the use of hired hands to assist in the labor was both a burden and a blessing. Watching over the hired help took the Shakers away from their "spiritual duties," and, invariably, the work of the additional help did not meet their high standards.

Archie Young, who worked for the Shakers in the 1920s and 1940s, recalls that this photograph was taken by Irving Greenwood. Brother Irving apparently repeatedly told the men to pile more hay onto the wagons, even when the men protested that the wagon might collapse. After Irving took the photograph, the men could not fit the wagon through the barn door, as the load of hay was too wide. It sat outside overnight and "exploded" the next morning.

Beverages[1]

"The Merrimack County Farm tour conducted by the Merrimack County Farmers Association visits our village. Four hundred and fifty people, men, women, and children, arrive at nine o'clock in the morning. Eighty-eight automobiles line up in our street. Grape juice and lemonade are served . . . "

—Josephine E. Wilson,
diary entry, August 30, 1916

We are often asked what beverages we serve at our table, and I think it might be interesting to explore this a little. As I am not able to research any of this, I am pulling on my memory cords to see just what I can remember was made throughout the years.

In the early days, Shakers had their own cider mill, so they had plenty of cider to put on the table. In my day, we had to take the apples to a nearby press, but we were provided amply because of the plentiful amount of apples we had. I think I have read in the accounts that, at one time, the Brothers were allowed a pint of cider each day, and the Sisters only a half pint. The Shakers eventually put a stop to the drinking of it because they found out that some of the Brothers were drinking it after it had gone by. Of course, we made our own cider vinegar, so it wasn't wasted.

Some of the old-fashioned recipes are very, very good. When I was young, we made a drink from sassafras and checkerberry leaves. We would steep them for quite a while and then add yeast with sugar to make a delicious cold drink.

Catnip tea was also made quite a good deal here. This drink is very helpful to people with nervous troubles or colds. A cup of catnip tea seemed to cure the cold in hardly any time.

A drink that was widely used by our haymakers was hop beer. We called it just the "hop drink," but it really was a beer, as the basis for all beers is hops. Our hops grew on the north and east fence of the Apiary. I think Sister Julia Briggs planted them in the years gone by, and they're still bearing occasionally. We had a very nice vine by the Carpenters' Shop, too. The hops would keep for years. We would dry them and use them at any time. I had buckets of dry hops so that in my day we made it for ourselves as well and could have it out of the hops season. We would put the hops on the back of the stove and let them steep in boiling water, then drain them off and add a certain amount of sugar or honey to taste. Then this was put to fermenting, and we would add yeast. It made an effervescent, very delicious, and cooling drink in hot weather.

Another beverage was made from cocoa shells. The Shakers would buy the shells by the pound, so the Sisters could have the shells to steep whenever they wanted. Sister Aida Elam liked the drink very much. She would put the shells into boiling water and steep them out, just like tea leaves, and then she would add sugar. The shells made quite a nice drink before we had a lot of cocoa on hand.

The Shakers would also buy for the children a substance called "Drink It." I imagine that it was made from a cereal foundation. It gave the children something they could actually enjoy during the cold season.

The Shakers planted the cranberry bush in years gone by down by our Turning Mill Pond, the Ice Mill Pond (see plates 6, 7, and 8), and the island in Runaway Pond. These bushes eventually failed, but in my young days, we were able to gather a few cranberries from the lingering bushes that still clung to the ground. The Shakers also planted the high-bush cranberry. Shakers from other communities used the berries to make a medicine called "vibernum." We found that the berries made a very delicious nerve tonic. We used to go up in the fall and pick the red, flat berries, and Sister Rebecca and I would make a drink for the Family from them. We'd boil the berries until they were cooked soft, and then we'd put them through a strainer. We used to put the berries in a bag to make the juice come out nice and clear, and then we'd add a certain amount of sugar, according to taste.

Many, many grapes were planted in areas in our home. I can well remember the grapevines that grew in the North Orchard. Sister Julia took care of them, and the grape arbors were put up on at least three terraces. Sister Julia planted the Diamond grapevines, and later, Mildred and I planted the Concord grape, a most favorite grape of all, and the Caro, a white grape, by Enfield House. Muscadines were planted for eating, and I can remember the walls of the cow lane leading down to the ponds being lined on both sides with Frost grapevines. Those grapes were small and dark and made a very rich, good juice. We would take these grapes in the fall, and we used to boil them down full strength. We just covered them with water and boiled them until they were soft. We had heavy bags of wooly material like flannel, and put them on frames in the Syrup Shop. We would pour the berries into the bags and let them drip all night, sometimes, to strain the juice out of them. We used to add eight quarts of this clear grape juice to four pounds of sugar. In this way, the liquid was condensed, so when we took it out to use as a drink, we would dilute it by half. We would make nine or ten quarts of our famous grape juice this way. Many times in the summer, in the earlier days, our guests—the tourists who came here— would be served a quart of our grape juice. We didn't expect them to pay for it, either; they were given the drink because it made a delightful, cooling beverage in hot weather, and we were very happy to have them enjoy the fruit of the vine as we did. We also used the grape juice for our grape sponge pudding (see page 82).

Although I do not consider wine a beverage, I would like to mention it as the Shakers made a good deal of wine and many varieties. Some of the best wines are homemade, I think. These were kept under the care of the Eldresses, who stored them in a three-cornered cupboard in the Sisters' Shop cellar. They were given to individuals as needed,

especially if the Brothers or Sisters had been out in the cold
and needed something to warm them up. We looked forward
to the spring months, when we would be cleaning the cellars,
for we knew that Eldress Dorothea Cochran would come
around with little, tiny glasses of blackberry wine for us to
have. It was chilly in the cellars, so springtime was when we
were happy to taste one of the most delicious wines.

I think one of the best was the dandelion wine. Dandelion
blossoms combined with oranges and lemons made this very
fine, golden wine. We also made elderberry wine. Around
our village many elderberry bushes grew, and there was
always a plentiful supply of berries to make wine and a very
delicious jelly. Raspberry wine was sometimes made, as we
also had many raspberry bushes around, some growing wild.
Later, Sister Rebecca had cultivated ones planted in the
north end of the vegetable garden.

Beverages also included a rhubarb drink, and, in later
years, herb drinks of many kinds. It is interesting to try them,
to find just the right combinations that are pleasing to the
taste. The recipes following are some of the beverages that
have been tested by the Shakers.

Cold Rhubarb Tea

4 cups rhubarb stalks (with   Rind of lemon or orange,
  red skin), unpeeled, diced   grated
4 cups water   ¾ cup sugar
Juice of 1 lemon or orange

Simmer rhubarb in water until very tender, about 20–
25 minutes. Strain. Add juice, rind, and sugar. Stir until
sugar has dissolved. Cool well and serve over ice in tall,
clear glasses.

Serves 4   —adapted from Amy Bess Miller and Persis
                                  Wellington Fuller, Best of Shaker Cooking

Herbade #2

1½ quarts boiling water   1 quart tea (strong)
1 cup lemon balm   1 cup sugar
2 cups borage   1 cup water
1 cup mint   3 quarts ginger ale
Juice of 6 lemons   Mint leaves (fresh)
Juice of 2 oranges

Pour boiling water over lemon balm. Steep 20 minutes. Strain onto borage and mint leaves. Add juices, tea, and syrup made of sugar and water. Let stand overnight or at least 8 hours. Strain. Add ice and ginger ale and fresh mint leaves at the last moment.

Serves 12
—adapted from Amy Bess Miller and Persis Wellington Fuller, *Best of Shaker Cooking*

Herb Tea

2 quarts water, boiling
½ cup goldenrod blossoms[2]
½ cup borage
½ cup mint
½ cup lemon balm
Honey, to taste

Add herbs to boiling water and let set 8 hours. Strain and chill. Add honey right before serving. Goldenrod is good for those people with arthritis.

Serves 8–10
—Bertha Lindsay's notes, Shaker Archives, SVI

Shaker Mint Cup

½ cup sugar
2 cups water
Dash salt
2 cups mint leaves,
    finely cut

2 quarts ginger ale
1 quart white grape juice
    (optional)
Sprigs of mint

Make a simple syrup by boiling the sugar and water 3 minutes. Add salt. Pour boiling syrup over the leaves. Let stand about 5 minutes. Add ginger ale. You will find the salt will help bring out the mint flavor of the leaves. Serve very cold. A sprig of mint helps pretty up this good drink. Eldress Gertrude Soule likes the grape juice as an addition.

Serves 8–12   —adapted from Mary Cass, Whitewater
                             Shaker Village, Amy Bess Miller and Persis
                             Wellington Fuller, *The Best of Shaker Cooking*

꙳

We made this drink for the haymakers.

Hop Drink

2½ gallons cold water
4 heaping teacups of hops
1½ quarts sugar
¼ yeast cake

Steep hops in water on side of stove (over low heat) for several hours, then strain. Cool until lukewarm. Add sugar and yeast. Bottle.

Makes 3 gallons   —Bertha Lindsay's scrapbook

Another drink that was popular with our haymakers was switchel; they said there was nothing more cooling. (See plate 32.)

Switchel

4 cups brown sugar
2 cups molasses
2 teaspoons ginger
2 gallons water
2 cups vinegar

Stir all ingredients together. Chill and serve. (Can be served over ice.)

Serves 32   —Quoted to the editor, 1986

AFTERWORD

*I*t has been a very happy experience for me to live under the influence of such beautiful people, and I hope that my last days will be a benefit and a blessing to all who come in contact with me. It is my desire to further the Shaker religion in any way that I can, and if I can influence young people to take Jesus Christ as their Savior, it will be worth all the effort.

I would like to add that the girls we took care of—Rosamond, Alberta, Eleanor, Helen, Hazel—all still correspond with us, and come to see us when they can, which is so rewarding after taking care of them for so many years.

The Shakers are being honored throughout the country at this time. There are many exhibits and many shows in different places honoring the ones who made the furniture. But the furniture will not last as long as the philosophy of the Shakers, and I am proud that I have been a part of this culture and perhaps in my small way can add a little bit to people's happiness by what I can say or do for them.

The Canterbury Shakers, who prided themselves on their industries, were also agrarian out of necessity. The fertile ground provided abundantly for our needs, and we can truthfully say with the Psalmist of old:

> *He watereth the hills from his chambers: the earth*
> *is satisfied with the fruit of thy works.*
> *He causeth the grass to grow for the cattle,*
> *and herb for the service of man: that he may*
> *bring forth food out of the earth,*
> *And wine that maketh glad the heart of man*
> *and oil to make his face to shine,*
> *and bread which strengtheneth man's heart.*

Ps. 104:13–15.

— *Eldress Bertha Lindsay*

Plate 33.   Shucking corn in the Syrup Shop, south wall, south room, first floor, c. 1929. *Shaker Archives, 1–PN544, SVI.*

When it was time to harvest the produce, Rebecca Hathaway, Kitchen Deaconess, called on many of the Sisters to help. The older Sisters sat together, about fifteen at a time, cutting the fruits and vegetables. As part of their training, the girls would trot back and forth, clearing away trays of parings and replacing them with trays of fresh produce. The young ones had to work fast, Bertha remembers, so as to avoid keeping an older Sister waiting.

BIOGRAPHIES OF
CANTERBURY SHAKERS[1]

BLINN, HENRY CLAY. Elder Henry was born in Providence, Rhode Island, in 1824. At fourteen, he entered the Canterbury Shaker Society and signed the covenant in 1846.[2] Elder Henry took up several trades at the village, including bee keeping, teaching, and printing (including the Shaker periodical *The Manifesto*). In 1852 Elder Henry was appointed to the order of the Elders and was placed in the Ministry. A prolific writer and researcher, Elder Henry recorded the history of the New Hampshire Shaker Societies and wrote a biography of Mother Ann Lee. He died in 1905.

BRIGGS, JULIA JANE. Sister Julia was born in Providence, Rhode Island, in 1844. She entered the Society with her mother and two brothers in 1852. In 1866 she signed the covenant. She succeeded Amanda Mathews as the Laundry Sister. Her other duties included raising grapes and making bonnets. She died in 1930.

BRUCE, ARTHUR. Elder Arthur was born in Springfield, Massachusetts, in 1858. He entered the Society in 1885 and signed the covenant two years later. He oversaw the planting of the vegetables and kept meticulous records of the cattle. An excellent financier, he was appointed Trustee in 1892, Elder in 1899, and Lead Minister in 1919. He died of pneumonia in 1938.

CLARK[E], EDITH PATIA ["EUNICE"]. Sister Eunice was born in East Providence, Rhode Island, in 1891 and entered the Society in 1905. She signed the covenant in 1912. A good seamstress, Eunice worked in the cloak and sweater industries. She played a saxophone in the Canterbury Shaker orchestra and helped Sister Ida Crook with Trustee duties. Eunice sometimes worked in the Office kitchen and helped sell the baked beans and brown bread, but cooking was not a favorite activity of hers. She died of cancer in 1957.

COCHRAN, ALEXANDER. Alexander was born in Glasgow, Scotland, in 1849. He entered the Society in 1857 and helped design a method of drying the Shakers' apples. He left the community in 1890.

COCHRAN, DOROTHEA T. Eldress Dorothea was born in Duntalker, Scotland, in 1844. She entered the Society in 1857 and signed the covenant in 1866. In 1898 she succeeded Dorothy Durgin as Eldress. Dorothea was especially fond of Bertha and referred to her as her "golden child." Eldress Dorothea died in 1912.

COOK, DAISY ELLA. Sister Ella was born in Providence, Rhode Island, in 1872. She entered the Society in 1885 and signed the covenant in 1893. Eldress Bertha remembers her as a "wonderful cook." She took care of the young girls and sang in the Canterbury Shakers' Echo Quartet. Sister Ella died in 1933.

CROOK, IDA F[RANCES]. Eldress Ida was born in Valley Falls, Rhode Island, in 1886. She entered the Society in 1897 with Lena Crook when she was eleven years old. Ida signed the covenant in 1908. She loved children, and at age nineteen, became associate teacher, working with Ella Cook and Aida Elam. (See plate 27.) Ida frequently worked in the bakery and taught some of the Sisters how to make pies. A gifted seamstress, she made dresses for the girls and worked with Josephine Wilson sewing hundreds of aprons for sale. She eventually became Trustee of the community and Associate Minister of the United Society. Ida died in 1965.

CROOK, LENA. Sister Lena was born in Pawtucket, Rhode Island, in 1889. She entered the Society in 1897 and signed the covenant in 1910. She worked on the knitting machines for the Canterbury Sisters' sweater industry and was known as a good bread maker. Lena left the community in 1920.

CROOKER, A. JANE. Sister Jane was born in Tamworth, New Hampshire, in 1834 and entered the Canterbury community in 1837. She signed the covenant in 1856. Sister Jane worked in the Creamery, and one of her duties was to make butter at the community. She died in 1916.

CURTIS, GERTNA, EDNA [EDNA G.] Sister Gertna was born in West Topsham, Vermont, in 1881. She entered the Society in 1899 and signed the covenant in 1902. She taught Bertha how to make bread. She was also a good pianist. Gertna left the Society in 1917.

DURGIN, DOROTHY ANN. Eldress Dorothy was born in Sanbornton, New Hampshire, in 1825. She entered the Society in 1834 and signed the covenant in 1848. Eldress Dorothy was a strong believer in distributing authority equally among the male and female leaders. About 1890, she designed a cloak from which copies were made and sold not only at Canterbury but at other Shaker communities as well. She served as Eldress for forty-six years until her death in 1898.

ELAM, AIDA M. Sister Aida was born in Providence, Rhode Island, in 1882. She entered the Society in 1893 and signed the covenant in 1903. Gifted in several areas, Aida taught school, played the cello, and directed the "entertainments" at the village. She frequently worked in the Dwelling House kitchen and taught some of the Sisters how to cook. Aida was one of the Sisters who sold the baked beans, brown bread, and pickles in Concord. (See plates 15, 27.) She died of cancer in 1962.

EVANS, JR., JESSIE. Sister Jessie was born in Liverpool, England, in 1867. She entered the Society in 1881 and signed the covenant seven years later. For many years, she was the community's schoolteacher, librarian, and nurse. She died of heart disease in 1937.

FISH, JENNIE H. Eldress Jennie was born in Bristol, Rhode Island, in 1857. She entered the Society in 1865 and signed the covenant in 1879. In 1912, she went to Ohio to help care for the elderly Sisters at Union Village and stayed there three years. She sang in the Canterbury Shakers' *Que Vive* Quartet and served as Deaconess and briefly as Eldress. In 1920 she died of Bright's disease.

FITTS, EDNA [EDNAH] E. Eldress Edna was born in the town of Canterbury, New Hampshire, east of the Shaker community, in 1846. She was taken to the Shakers as an infant, and she signed the covenant when she was twenty-two. Edna served as Trustee and became Lead Minister in 1911. She died of cancer in 1924.

FLETCHER, DANIEL. Brother Daniel was born in Dunstable, Massachusetts, in 1764 and was one of the first to help settle the Canterbury Shaker community. In 1811, he moved to the North Family and ran the farm there. Six years later, he returned to the Church Family and took care of the vegetable garden. He died in 1816.

FROST, ETHEL NEAL. Sister Ethel was born in Peabody, Massachusetts, in 1898 and entered the Society in 1903. She signed the covenant in 1919. Ethel Frost worked in all of the Sisters' trades, including the very specialized work of weaving bonnet braids. She left the community in 1923.

FULLER, JOHN. Brother John was born in Maine in 1765 and entered the Society in 1792, the year the community was established. Elder Henry Blinn described him as "a minister of spiritual life in all the seasons of worship." Brother John was one of the first people to tend the Canterbury Shakers' vegetable garden, and he was appointed Assistant Elder in 1803. He died in 1837.

GARDNER, BLANCH[E] L. Sister Blanche was born in New York City in 1873 and entered the Society in 1881. She signed the covenant in 1894. In 1939 she was appointed Trustee and worked with Eldress Josephine Wilson in the Office. She served as bookkeeper, helped make the cloaks, and shipped out the sale items. Blanche also served as "overseer" of the Office cooks, distributing the canned goods that were stored and communicating the shopping needs to Elder Arthur Bruce. She died in 1945.

GREEN, EDITH M. Sister Edith was born in Gloucester, Massachusetts, in 1879. Her father was from the West Indies and her mother was from Maine. Edith entered the Society in 1895 and signed the covenant in 1914. She worked on the sweaters, made hat brushes, and crocheted goods for sale. She also went on sales trips and worked in the Creamery. She helped harvest berries and prepared the vegetables for canning. (See plates 9, 22, 26.) She died in 1951.

GREENWOOD, ELMER IRVING. Brother Irving was born in Providence, Rhode Island, in 1876. He entered the community ten years later and signed the covenant in 1897. Having exceptional mechanical skills, he installed electrical wiring throughout the village in 1910. The Shakers relied on him a great deal in keeping their equipment maintained and providing up-to-date radios and automobiles. (See plate 6.) Irving became Lead Minister in 1933 and died in 1939, the last Brother to live at Canterbury.

HATHAWAY, REBECCA. Sister Rebecca was born in Providence, Rhode Island, in 1872. She entered the Society when she was ten years old and signed the covenant in 1893. Gradually her role in the community grew as Sisters died, left, or were assigned to other duties. In 1912 she took over Jennie Fish's charge as Kitchen Deaconess. After Amy Sargent died in 1920, she also supervised the manufacture of confections for sale. About this time, she inherited Amanda Mathews' duty of canning the produce. When Bertha was learning how to cook, Rebecca was in charge of the garden harvest. She taught Bertha canning, pickling, and the basics of cooking. (See plates 8, 19, 31.) Sister Rebecca died in 1958.

HEWITT, MARY ALICE ["MURIEL"]. Muriel was born in 1900. She entered the community in 1913 and grew up at the village with three other sisters in her family. She signed the covenant in 1921. Muriel assisted Sister Rebecca in the canning and pickling, and helped with the cooking in the Trustees' Office and the harvesting of produce. (See plates 15, 19.) Muriel left the community about 1930.

HOWLAND, ALICE MIRIAM. Sister Alice was born in 1884 in Lowell, Massachusetts, and entered the Society in 1899. She lived at the Second Family until it disbanded and then moved to the

Church Family where she spent the rest of her life. She signed the covenant in 1914. Alice taught Ethel Hudson the basics of cooking and remained her close friend. A gifted artist, she decorated note cards for the Shakers to sell. She also took care of the bees at the village. Alice died in 1973.

HUDSON, ETHEL MARY. Sister Ethel was born in Salem, Massachusetts, in 1897 and entered the Canterbury community in 1907. Initially, she lived at the Second Family and helped take care of the remaining elderly Sisters there until that Family disbanded. She moved to the Church Family in 1917 and signed the covenant two years later. Sister Ethel learned how to cook at the Second Family. She later served as pastry cook at the bakery and Office kitchen and as messer at the Dwelling House kitchen. She lives at the village today and maintains a private life there. (See plate 22.)

KING, EMMA BELL. Eldress Emma was born in 1873 in Providence, Rhode Island, and entered the Society in 1878. In 1894 she signed the covenant. In 1918 Emma became Eldress in the Church Family and served in that position until her death in 1966. She taught in the Canterbury Shaker school for many years and was an intellectual leader of the Canterbury Shakers and other societies. Beginning in 1947, she served as Lead Minister and was a dominant figure in the Ministry from 1957 until her death. (See plates 11, 21.)

LINDSAY, GOLDIE INA RUBY ["BERTHA"]. Eldress Bertha was born in Braintree, Massachusetts, in 1897. The following year, she and her family returned to their home in Laconia, New Hampshire. In 1905 she was placed as an orphan in the care of the Canterbury Shakers, and she signed the covenant when she was twenty-one. Eldress Bertha's main activities at the village revolved around the harvesting, processing, and serving of food. She was also in charge of the fancywork trade from 1944 to 1958. In 1967 she was appointed as Canterbury Eldress and as a member of the Lead Ministry. Eldress Bertha was instrumental in the decision to convey the deed of the Canterbury site and properties to Shaker Village, Inc., a nonprofit educational institution. Today she greets visitors, grants interviews, records her memoirs, and plans meals. As honorary President of the Board of Trustees of Shaker Village,

Inc., she plays an active role in the preservation and research of the site. (See plates 1, 3, 8, 12, 16, 19, 22, 26.)

MATHEWS, AMANDA A. Sister Amanda was born in Providence, Rhode Island, in 1847. She entered the Society in 1856 and signed the covenant in 1868. Sister Amanda was in charge of preserving the fruits and vegetables and taught the trade to Sister Rebecca. She died in 1913.

OTIS, JAMES M. Brother James was born in Portsmouth, New Hampshire, in 1817. He entered the Society in 1831. In 1842 he was moved to the Office as Trustee. One of his duties was to take care of the vegetable garden in the Church Family. He left the community in 1845.

PARMENTER, ELEANOR EVELYN. Eleanor was born in Worcester, Massachusetts, in 1913 and entered the community in 1926. She worked for Bertha for a short while in the Office kitchen and later assisted Evelyn Polsey in the sale of the baked beans in Concord. She left the community in 1940. (See plate 13.)

PHELPS, BERTHA LILLIAN. Sister Lillian was born in East Boston, Massachusetts, in 1876. She entered the Society in 1892 and signed the covenant in 1899. Sister Lillian was Bertha's best friend. (See plate 31.) She made items for sale in the gift shop and was involved in the sweater trade. One of her duties was to work as the third cook in the Dwelling House kitchen. In 1918, Lillian was appointed Second Eldress, and in 1965 she became Office Sister. She died in 1973.

PHELPS, FLORENCE ETHEL. Sister Florence was born in Roxbury, Massachusetts, in 1879. She entered the Society in 1893, and signed the covenant seven years later. Florence worked in the Dwelling House kitchen, assisted in the harvesting of the fruits and vegetables, and worked in the Laundry. She left the community in 1922. (See plates 22, 26.)

POLSEY S. EVELYN. Sister Evelyn was born in Pawtucket, Rhode Island, in 1891. She entered the Society in 1902 and signed the covenant in 1912. Sister Evelyn helped Bertha with the canning, served as a head cook at the Dwelling House, and was involved with the sale of the baked beans. Evelyn died in 1955. (See plates 17, 27, 29.)

ROBERTS, ALICE GERTRUDE. Gretrude was born in 1903 in Attleboro Falls, Massachusetts. She entered the Society with her sisters when she was thirteen and signed the covenant in 1924. She helped in the fancywork trade and worked in the Dwelling House kitchen. She left the community in 1935. (See plate 29.)

ROWELL LEONA MERRILL. Leona was born in 1905 in Standish, Maine, and entered the Canterbury community in 1913. In 1926 she signed the covenant. She worked in the bakery and in the Office kitchen, mainly as second cook. She also served as third cook and assisted in the dining rooms at the Dwelling House. She learned to make pies from Ida Crook and how to make bread from Helena Sarle. Leona left the community in 1935. (See plate 8.)

SARGENT, ANNIE MAY ["AMY"]. Sister Amy was born in 1883 in Manchester, New Hampshire. She entered the Society when she was eight years old and signed the covenant on her twenty-first birthday. Sister Amy had the charge of the confections that were sold to the public. She later trained Sister Rebecca Hathaway. Eldress Bertha has fond memories of Amy: "She was a very gifted Sister and wrote many of the plays which we gave to the Family. One which stands in my memory particularly, which was given on an Easter day, was *The Walk to Emmaus*. The play was beautifully written and explained the relationship of the disciples with Christ. . . . " Sister Amy died of tuberculosis in 1920.

SARLE, CORA HELENA. Sister Helena was born in North Scituate, Massachusetts, in 1867. She entered the Society in 1882 when she was fifteen and signed the covenant six years later. Sister Helena is remembered today as a landscape artist, but she was known as "Grammy" to the young girls who lived at the village. She was Bertha's friend for many years and comforted her when she first arrived at the village in 1905. Sister Helena crocheted beautifully and baked delicious pies and breads. When the Shakers had popcorn parties, she and Rebecca Hathaway helped the young people make candy. She died in 1956. (See plate 30.)

SHEPARD, LUCY. Lucy Shepard was born in 1836 and entered the Society when she was almost eleven years old. She signed the covenant in 1857. In 1891 she became Trustee, and with

Emeline Hart (1834–1914) formed the firm "Hart and Shepard" for the Canterbury Shakers. Under that name, many articles—sweaters, confections, the "Dorothy" cloak, and others—were sold. Lucy died in 1926.

SOULE, GERTRUDE MAY. Eldress Gertrude was born in Topsham, Maine, in 1894. She entered the Sabbathday Lake, Maine, community about 1906 and signed the covenant in 1915. She became an Eldress at Sabbathday Lake in 1950. Seven years later, she was selected as a member of the Lead Ministry and came to Canterbury to live in 1971. Today Eldress Gertrude greets visitors and aids researchers of Shaker culture and crafts. She serves as Second Vice President on the Board of Trustees of Shaker Village, Inc., which maintains the Canterbury Shaker Church Family site. As Lead Minister she represents the United Society in official business and public functions.

VICKERY, HOPE BRADFORD. Sister Hope was born in Providence, Rhode Island, in 1881. She entered the Society in 1894 and signed the covenant in 1902. She helped teach Bertha how to make bread. Hope left the community in 1924.

WALL, GLADYS MIRIAM. Sister Miriam was born in Boston, Massachusetts, in 1896. She entered the Society in 1908 and signed the covenant in 1917. She sang duets with Bertha over the years and periodically served as head cook in the Dwelling House. In 1965 she was appointed Trustee. She died of cancer in 1977. (See plates 12, 27, 30.)

WEEKS, FRIEDA VINETTA. Sister Frieda was born in Palmer, Massachusetts, in 1891. She entered the Society in 1903 and signed the covenant nine years later. Sister Frieda helped with the fancywork trade and the harvesting. She left the community in 1935. (See plate 27.)

WELLS, ELLA ELEANOR ["MILDRED"]. Mildred was born in 1904 in Everett, Massachusetts, and lived on Shaker soil most of her life. She arrived at the Canterbury community in 1921 and, until her death in May of 1987, maintained an active, although private, life at the village. An excellent cook, she frequently worked with Miriam Wall in the Dwelling House kitchen and with Bertha in the Office kitchen.

WHITCHER, MARY. Eldress Mary was born in Laurens, New Jersey in 1815. She entered the Canterbury Society in 1826 and signed the covenant ten years later. Her father had donated the land that became known as the Church Family. From 1859 to 1865 she served as Minister to oversee the Canterbury and Enfield communities. About 1882 she endorsed *Mary Whitcher's Shaker House-Keeper*, a cookbook that advertised the Canterbury Shaker sarsaparilla syrup and other medicines distributed by Weeks and Potter of Boston. She died in 1890.

WILSON, JOSEPHINE E. Josephine was born in Lynn, Massachusetts, in 1866. She entered the Society in 1875 with her parents and sister. She lived at the Second Family for a while and later moved to the Church Family where she spent the rest of her life. In 1887 she signed the covenant. In 1918 she became a Trustee and proved her skills as a businesswoman and leader. She took charge of the manufacture of the "Dorothy" cloaks, organized the Sisters' fancywork sales trips, and helped with the printing of *The Manifesto*. Always interested in modernizing the Shakers' environment for efficiency and comfort, Sister Josephine was responsible for many renovations made in the Trustees' Office and in the Dwelling House. When Bertha was nineteen, she called her to cook at the Office. In 1939 Josephine became a member of the Lead Ministry. She died in 1946.

WILSON, MARY ANN. Eldress Mary was born in Portsmouth, New Hampshire, in 1863. She entered the Society in 1875 and lived at the Second Family for a short while. In 1884, she signed the covenant. About five years later, she was appointed Eldress. She worked on the cloak industry with Miriam Wall. Eldress Mary died in 1944.

WILSON, MARY LOUISA. Sister Mary was born in Leroy, Iowa, in 1858. (She was not related to Eldress Mary.) She entered the Canterbury community in 1869 and signed the covenant Christmas day, 1879. In 1887 she was appointed Trustee. She died in 1939.

NOTES

The abbreviation "SVI" refers to Shaker Archives, Shaker Village, Inc., Canterbury, New Hampshire.

PREFACE

1. One exception is *Shaker Your Plate,* a cookbook written by Sister Frances Carr, Sabbathday Lake Shaker, published by the University Press of New England, Hanover, New Hampshire.

2. The Canterbury Shakers, *Gourmet's Delight: Favorite Shaker Recipes* (Canterbury, New Hampshire, c. 1968); The Canterbury Shakers, *Shaker Tested Recipes* (Canterbury, New Hampshire, c. 1965); Mary Whitcher, *Mary Whitcher's Shaker House-Keeper* (Boston: Weeks & Potter, c. 1882) [Hereafter *House-Keeper*].

3. The other active Shaker community is Sabbathday Lake in New Gloucester, Maine.

4. The three monologues are recorded on tapes E25–28, made between 1984 and 1985 and cover Eldress Bertha's introduction and most of her chapters with recipes. Tape recordings E5–7 helped supplement the chapters on omelets, vegetables, and confections. Tapes E48 and E31 helped supply additional material for the chapters on puddings and beverages. Biographical material was found in the Canterbury Shakers' Biography File, Ms. 786 and tape recordings E7–9 and E49–50.

IDENTIFYING THE SHAKERS

1. Excellent discussions about Shaker religious beliefs include Marjorie Proctor-Smith, *Women in Shaker Community and Worship: A Feminist Analysis of the Uses of Religious Symbolism* (Lewiston, Maine: The Edwin Mellon Press, 1985) and Priscilla J. Brewer, *Shaker Communities, Shaker Lives* (Hanover, N.H.: University Press of New England, 1986) [Hereafter *Shaker Communities*].

2. A list of those communities and their years of existence can be found in Brewer, *Shaker Communities.*

3. A good summary of the social organization appears in June Sprigg, *Shaker Design* (New York: W. W. Norton & Company, 1986).

4. Henry C. Blinn, "A Historical Record of the Society of Believers in Canterbury, N.H. from the Time of its Organization in 1792 till the year one thousand eight hundred and forty-eight," Ms. 763, p. 10, SVI [Hereafter "Historical Record"].

DIETARY TRADITIONS OF THE CANTERBURY SHAKERS

1. Blinn, "Historical Record," p. 145.

2. Blinn, "Historical Record," p. 22.

3. The Canterbury Shakers planted several orchards at the village, beginning in 1795 with the North Orchard, which covered six acres. See Blinn, "Historical Record," p. 52. They planted the Moses Orchard in 1840, the Mill Orchard in 1848, the East Farm Orchard, the Union Orchard in 1855, and the Blacksmith Shop Orchard in 1881. In 1917 the New Orchard was set out in the Meeting House Field.

4. The Canterbury Shakers built a horse-drawn saw mill and gristmill in 1797. Three years later, they constructed a water-powered gristmill. This mill was replaced by another water-powered mill in 1832. An excellent description of the Canterbury Shaker mill system can be found in David R. Starbuck, "The Shaker Mills in Canterbury, New Hampshire," *The Journal for Industrial Archeology* 12, no. 1 (1986), pp. 11–38.

5. John Whitcher, et al., "A Brief History or Record of the Commencement & Progress of the United Society of Believers, at Canterbury. County of Merrimack. And. State of New Hampshire," Ms. 21, p. 21, SVI [Hereafter "History"].

6. Excellent sources that compare Shaker cuisine to traditional American cooking are Marcia Hartwell, "Comparison of Shaker Food to the Outside World's (Nineteenth Century)," *The Shaker Messenger* 5, no. 2 (Winter 1983): 10–11 [Hereafter "Shaker Food"] and Brewer, *Shaker Communities,* pp. 106–113, 131–134.

7. Blinn, "Historical Record," p. 145.

8. Brewer, *Shaker Communities,* p. 39. According to Brewer, the communications regarding any regulations prior to 1821 were always verbal. She states that in 1800 the New Lebanon Church Family leaders decided to use liquor for medicinal purposes only but wrote no instructions to members. Blinn recorded, "Historical Record," p. 121, that in September of

that year, "the Church agreed to deny themselves of the use of ardent spirits as drink, and [use] it only for medicinal purposes and by the advice of the Physicians."

9. Theodore E. Johnson, "The 'Millennial Laws' of 1821," *The Shaker Quarterly* 7, no. 2 (Summer 1967), pp. 47–48, 51, 55.

10. Blinn, "Historical Record," p. 214.

11. Ibid.

12. Ibid, p. 251.

13. Ibid, p. 252.

14. Letter of Ministry Canterbury to Ministry New Lebanon, Jan. 20, 1836, WRHS IV A4, as seen in Brewer, *Shaker Communities,* p. 109.

15. Blinn, "Historical Record," p. 252.

16. Ibid, p. 280. According to Blinn, pp. 22–23, the drink made from "Avens" was considered "excellent for the system." When served with milk and sugar, it was supposed to taste like chocolate. Brewer, *Shaker Communities,* pp. 106, 131, believes that the issue of vegetarianism was one of the most divisive disputes experienced by the Shakers in the nineteenth century.

17. Elder H[enry] C. Blinn, "Church Record, 1784–1879," Ms. 764, p. 40, SVI [Hereafter "Church Record"].

18. An analysis of the Canterbury Shaker herbal catalogues is in unpublished research by Galen Beale, SVI.

19. Blinn, "Historical Record," p. 252.

20. Hartwell, "Shaker Food," pp. 10–11.

21. Blinn, "Church Record," p. 101; Whitcher, "History," p. 299.

INTRODUCTION BY ELDRESS BERTHA LINDSAY

1. Bertha Lindsay, Monologue. [1984.] Tape Recording E25, SVI [Hereafter E25].

2. Eldress Bertha's mother was Abbie N. Smith. She and her husband, Lloyd E. Lindsay, and their nine children lived in Laconia, New Hampshire. Both Bertha's parents died when she was four, and in 1905 she was brought to the Canterbury Shaker community as an orphan.

3. Shaker Sisters, since the mid-nineteenth century, were active in the manufacture and sale of a variety of goods. By the late nineteenth century, the Sisters sold the items both on and off the site. Over the years, until about 1944, two or three Sisters would take sales trips together and would be gone for several weeks at a time. As with the other duties, this work was rotated. The Canterbury Shakers' last main industry, the fancywork trade, closed in 1958.

4. One book is a late nineteenth-century geography textbook
   that was probably used by school children at the village
   before Bertha took it over to store her favorite recipes. She
   refers to the book as her "Geography." The other is a
   notebook that she began using in 1938. It was first used by
   Leona Merrill Rowell, who wrote instructions and recipes in
   it until she left in 1935. Bertha calls it her "Scrapbook."

Soups and Stews

1. Lindsay, E25.
2. Traditionally, Brothers tended the vegetable gardens. John
   Fuller (1765–1816) and Daniel Fletcher (1764–1837) were
   probably the first Brothers at the village who had the
   responsibility of managing the three- acre lot.

Meats, Poultry, and Fish

1. Lindsay, E25; Bertha Lindsay, Monologue. November 1985.
   Tape recording E28, SVI [Hereafter E28].
2. The Ice Mill Pond, also known as Factory Pond and Wood
   Mill Pond, was one of several connected to power the
   Canterbury Shakers' mills. It was created by the Shakers in
   1802 and housed a threshing mill and an ice house in the
   twentieth century. The ice house was "torn out" in 1929 due
   to the use of electric refrigeration at the village. The building
   was used for storage until it was removed from the site in
   1952. Elmer Irving Greenwood, Notebook, Ms. 28, SVI.
3. Chestnut trees were recorded at the village as early as 1817.
   In November, 1924, the Canterbury Shakers sold all of their
   chestnut timber. See Whitcher, "History," p. 107.

Casseroles

1. Lindsay, E25.
2. At that time the Sisters who lived and worked in the Office
   were Josephine Wilson, Lead Minister; Blanche Gardner,
   Trustee; and Mary Louisa Wilson, Postmaster.

Omelets

1. Bertha Lindsay, Monologue. 1978. Tape recording E5, SVI;
   Lindsay, E28.
2. Meeting House. In 1837 the Dwelling House was
   remodelled to provide a new "meeting room" because the
   Meeting House had become too crowded. Having the
   meeting room, or chapel, as it became known, in the
   Dwelling House was more convenient for the older members
   of the Society. See Penelope Watson, "A Building History,"
   The Canterbury Shakers 3 no. 1 (January 1983): 7.

Vegetables

1. Bertha Lindsay, Monologue. 1978. Tape recording E6, SVI [Hereafter E6]; Lindsay, E25; Bertha Lindsay, Monologue. [1984.] Tape recording E26, SVI [Hereafter E26].

2. In addition to their farmland on the family grounds, the Shakers purchased acreage elsewhere for various uses. They called the area "Intervale" because it is located on the plain, or intervale, of the Merrimack River. The land is located across the river from, and east of, downtown Concord.

3. The Canning House was built in 1797 and was moved to its present site west of the Laundry in 1841. It has also been known as the Granary, the Distillery, and finally, the Syrup Shop.

4. The oven described here was installed in the bakery around 1878. Revolving circular shelves inside the oven allowed the Shakers to bake great quantities of bread, pies, and other foods at the same time. The Canterbury Shakers wrote about and advertised the superior quality of this oven. According to Blinn, "Church Record," p. 243, the pattern came from the Enfield, Connecticut, Shaker Community. According to oral tradition, the oven was designed by Sister Emeline Hart (1834– 1914) who moved from Enfield to Canterbury in 1886.

5. Fitch's Drug Store was located on Warren Street in the center of Concord.

Salads

1. Lindsay, E25; Conversation with the editor, March 1986.

Sauces and Dressings

1. Lindsay, E26.

2. Originally, the Shakers dried their apples using a stove in the Laundry. In 1852 the Shakers constructed their first building used specifically for drying the apples. The fruit was spread on racks of netting on frames. These were placed above a large stove. In 1880 a new method, designed by George Blanchard of Concord and Brother Alexander Cochran, was attempted. The stationary racks were replaced with ones that hung from a revolving frame suspended above a stove. The frame, made of eight rows of four racks each, was periodically turned by hand. According to Irving Greenwood, the new system cost the Shakers $559.50. The stove was heated to two hundred degrees, but a defect in the chimney caused a fire, and half the building burned. In 1890 the Boys' Shop was remodelled to serve as a dry house. This structure was located on the north side of the vegetable garden but was razed in 1938.

3. Leona Merrill Rowell adds: "In the summertime we had Astrachan apples which we used to make applesauce. And we had an apple called the 'Virgin apple,' and it made the most beautiful applesauce you ever saw. We made applesauce every day but Sunday. We'd peel and cut the apples in quarters and put them in a pan of water to keep them from turning brown. And then we'd bring the water to a boil. Then we'd dish the applesauce into pans and let it cool in the bakery. We served it morning and night." Leona Merrill Rowell, Interview. 2 March 1987. Tape recording E50, SVI [Hereafter E50].

Breads

1. Lindsay, E25, E26.

Puddings and Desserts

1. Bertha Lindsay, Interview by the editor. 26 February 1987. Tape recording E48, SVI.

2. The North Shop was used for storage, drying herbs, and making items for sale. The cooks' storeroom was located there and contained built-in bins for dried beans, peas, and other foods.

3. In the eighteenth and nineteenth centuries, cooks of the "World" preferred Irish moss, a seaweed, for making blancmange and other puddings. In the twentieth century, cornstarch was probably more commonly used in the "World."

Pies

1. Lindsay, E25, E26, E28.

Cakes

1. Lindsay, E25, E28; Bertha Lindsay, Conversation with editor. 11 February 1986, SVI.

2. Leona Merrill Rowell received a cake on her twenty-first birthday. It was a "yellow" cake with a "boiled" frosting (made of boiled sugar water and a beaten egg white). Sister Alice Howland "painted" a wreath of pansies on the white icing. Rowell, E50.

3. According to Mildred Wells, 10 March 1987, Miriam was an "all-round cook who could make any dish well." Bertha was frequently asked to work at the Trustees' Office kitchen because she was a "gourmet cook."

Cookies

1. Lindsay, E28.

Confections

1. Lindsay, E6, E28; Bertha Lindsay, Monologue. 1984. Tape recording E27, SVI.

2. Flag root comes from sweet flag, *Acorus calamus.* The roots were gathered when two or three years old, in late autumn or early spring, before the stalks were hollow. Flag has a spicy, lemon smell. It was used as a substitute for ginger, cinnamon, and nutmeg and was considered to aid digestion. See Mrs. Maud Grieve, *A Modern Herbal* (New York: Dover Publications, Inc., 1971).

3. Maple Grove was located about two miles southeast of the Church Family buildings. A "sap camp" was built there in 1863.

4. The production of maple sugar was an important activity at the villge. Elder Henry Blinn recorded that in 1850, a peak year for the Canterbury Shakers' maple products, 379 barrels of sap were gathered, and 2,214 pounds of sugar were produced.

5. St. Paul's School is a private Episcopal school located about twenty miles southwest of the village in Concord.

Beverages

1. Lindsay, E26, E27; Bertha Lindsay, Monograph, n.d. Tape recording E31, SVI.

2. There are more than eighty species of goldenrod. *Solidago odora* is the only one that is medicinally valuable. The Shakers sold the anise-flavored leaves which were used as a stimulant, a carminative, and a diaphoretic. See Joseph E. Meyer, *The Herbalist,* 19th ed. (s.l., s.n.): 1975.

BIOGRAPHIES

1. Biography File, Ms. 786, SVI; Bertha Lindsay, Monologue. 1978. Tape recordings E7, E8, E9, SVI; Ethel Hudson, Interview. 27 February 1987. Tape recording E49, SVI; Rowell, E50.

2. To "enter a Society" meant to arrive at a Shaker community to live. Unless otherwise indicated in the text, the Society referred to is the Canterbury Shaker community. A person "signed the covenant" when he or she was ready to make a commitment to the Shaker way of life. The tradition can be traced to the eighteenth century when some of the Shaker communities were established. The first covenant signed by the Canterbury Shakers is dated 1796.

BIBLIOGRAPHY

Blinn, Henry C. "Church Record, 1784–1879." Ms. 764, SVI.

———. "A Historical Record of the Society of Believers in Canterbury, N.H., from the Time of its Organization in 1792 till the year one thousand eight hundred and forty-eight." Ms. 763, SVI.

[Blinn, Henry C., et al.] "Church Records II, [Canterbury], 1872– 1889." Ms. 22, SVI.

Brewer, Priscilla J. *Shaker Communities, Shaker Lives*. Hanover, N.H.: University Press of New England, 1986.

Evans, Jessie. Diaries, Canterbury, N.H., 1905–1931. Ms. 1984.14–.15, Ms. 1985.6–.43, SVI.

Family Circle, Inc., *Family Circle Magazine* (December 1965).

Greenwood, Elmer Irving. Diaries, Canterbury N.H., 1915–1917. Ms. 270, SVI.

———. Notebook, Canterbury, N.H. Ms. 28, SVI.

Grieve, Mrs. Maud. *A Modern Herbal: the Medicinal, Culinary, Cosmetic, and Economic Properties, Cultivation, and Folk-lore of Herbs, Grasses, Fungae, Shrubs, & Trees, with All Their Modern Scientific Uses*. Ed. Mrs. C. F. Leyel. N.Y.: Dover Publications, 1971.

Hartwell, Marcia Byrom. "Comparison of Shaker Food to that of the Outside World's (Nineteenth Century)," *The Shaker Messenger* 5, no. 2 (Winter 1983).

———. "Ice Cream and the Shakers," *The Shaker Messenger* 5, no. 4 (Summer 1983), 12–25.

Hewitt, Mary Alice. Monologue. 3 September 1978. Tape Recording E12, SVI.

Hill, Isaac. *The Farmer's Monthly Visitor* 2, no. 3 (31 August 1840), SVI, 10–11.

"Historical Record of the Church Family, East Canterbury, N.H. Compiled by the Brethren for Special Reference. 1890–1930." Ms. 33, SVI.

Hudson, Ethel. Interview by editor. 27 February 1987. Tape Recording E49, SVI.

Johnson, Theodore E. "The 'Millennial Laws' of 1821." *The Shaker Quarterly* 7 (Summer 1967), pp. 35–58.

Kremer, Elizabeth C. *We Make You Kindly Welcome: Recipes from Trustees' House Daily Fare.* Lexington, Ky.: Pleasant Hill Press, 1970.

Lindsay, Bertha. Conversation with editor. 10 May 1985, SVI.

———. Conversation with editor. 13 November 1985, SVI.

———. Conversation with editor. 11 February 1986, SVI.

———. Conversation with editor. 20 May 1986, SVI.

———. Monologues. 1978. Tape Recordings E1, E3, E5–E9, SVI.

———. Monologues. [1984.] Tape Recordings E25, E26, E27, SVI.

———. Monologue. November 1985. Tape Recording E28, SVI.

———. Monologues. n.d. Tape Recordings E31, E32, SVI.

———. Monologue. 1986. Tape Recordings E38–E40, SVI.

———. Interview by editor. 26 February 1987. Tape Recording E48, SVI.

———. "Eldress Bertha Recalls the 1920s." *The Canterbury Shakers* 3, no. 1 (January 1983): 1–5.

———. Notes and Recipes. n.d. SVI.

———. Interviews by Charles "Bud" Thompson. 1981–1986. Tape Recordings E20, E21, SVI.

———. Scrapbook, 1938. Canterbury, New Hampshire. Collection of Bertha Lindsay.

———. Scrapbook, n.d. Canterbury, New Hampshire. Collection of Bertha Lindsay.

———. Scrapbook, "Geography," n.d. Canterbury, New Hampshire. Collection of Bertha Lindsay.

Meyer, Joseph E. *The Herbalist.* 19th ed. (s.l, s.n.): 1975.

Miller, Amy Bess Williams, and Persis Wellington Fuller. *The Best of Shaker Cooking.* N.Y.: The Macmillan Company, 1970.

"The 1929 Christmas Eve Program." Ms. 996, SVI.

Notebook, Canterbury, N.H. Ms. 969, SVI.

Pictorial Review Standard Cookbook: 1000 Tested Recipes, A Sure Guide for Every Bride. N.Y.: Pictorial Review Co., n.d.

Piercy, Caroline B. *The Shaker Cookbook: Not by Bread Alone.* N.Y.: Crown Publishers, Inc., 1953.

Rowell, Leona Merrill. Interview by editor. 2 March 1987. Tape Recording E50, SVI.

Safford, Marion F. "Shaker Sisters Victory Garden Has 45 Long Rows of Vegetables." *The Boston Globe,* 18 June 1944.

Shakers, The Canterbury. *Gourmet's Delight: Favorite Shaker Recipes.* Canterbury, N.H.: s.n., n.d.

———. *Shaker Tested Recipes: Favorite Shaker Recipes.* Canterbury, N.H.: s.n., n.d.

Showalter, Mary Emma. *Mennonite Community Cookbook: Favorite Family Recipes.* Philadelphia: The John C. Winston Company, 1950.

Starbuck, David R., ed. *Canterbury Shaker Village, An Historical Survey.* Vol. 2. Durham, N.H.: University of New Hampshire, 1981.

———. "The Shaker Mills at Canterbury, New Hampshire," *The Journal of the Society for Industrial Archeology* 12, no. 1 (1986): 11–38.

Starbuck, David R., and Margaret Supplee Smith, *Historical Survey of Canterbury Shaker Village.* Boston: Boston University, 1979.

Watson, Penelope. "A Building History." *The Canterbury Shakers* 3, no. 1 (January 1983): 7.

Whitcher, Mary. *Mary Whitcher's Shaker House-Keeper.* Boston: Weeks & Potter, n.d. [c. 1882].

Whitcher, John, et al. "A Brief History or Record of the Commencement & Progress of the United Society of Believers, at Canterbury. County of Merrimack. And. State of New Hampshire." Ms. 21, SVI.

Wilson, Josephine E. Diaries, Canterbury, N.H., 1916–1940. Ms. 1985.25, 1985.41–74, SVI.

[Winkley, Francis, et al.] Journal, Canterbury, N.H., 1784–1845. Ms. 25, SVI.

Young, Archie. Conversation with editor, 10 October 1983.

Recipes and Principal Ingredients

General Index